Kurdistan

Genocide and Rebirth

The destruction of Kurdistan
and its rebuilding

Davan Yahya Khalil

Davan Yahya Khalil
UK

First Edition 2013

Manufactured in the UK.

Publishers' Acknowledgements

Editorial: Davan Yahya Khalil
Project Co-ordinator: Demi Quinn
Typesetting: Su Quinn
Cover design: Chris Berry

Published by: The Writing Company

For the people of Kurdistan

Contents

Introduction

What is Kurdistan? It is a more difficult question to answer than it might sound at first. One of the hardest things for someone to do is to sum up a place. A region. Potentially an entire country. That is particularly true when it is a place they know well, because there is too much detail in what they know to ever sum it up in just a few words. Which details are the ones that will really capture the essence of a place? Which ones only skim the surface?

I could refer to some of the things that have been done to Kurdistan and my people, the Kurds, in the past. It is the way that so many people have viewed Kurdistan before, and it is the topic I intend to explore in this book. Yet to begin that way would be doing the region a disservice. It would mean that the only impression those readers who have never visited Kurdistan will get is of a region defined by the violence done to it, and that is not acceptable. Kurdistan is so much more than that.

So instead, let us begin with what a visitor to Kurdistan would see. Arriving either by air or travelling over the border by road, they would quickly find themselves at the heart of one of

Kurdistan's modern, prosperous cities. They would see the constant signs of building and probably note the wealth around them in many areas. Landing in Erbil or Sulaymaniyah, they could look around and think that they were in any of the world's major urban centres. They would see prosperous surroundings, safe, orderly environments, and the hectic pace of ordinary life the world over.

They could see all this, in what is currently a region of Iraq.

That's the dichotomy of Kurdistan. It has been in the middle of one of the most reported on conflicts on the planet, yet it is also a comparatively safe, booming region. It is a region that has, in a very short space of time, almost entirely reinvented itself. It is a region where there are new houses and projects going up every day, and where strong natural resources provide the potential for future growth. There are even those who are starting to refer to it as a potential 'second Dubai'. All that, in an area of the world that continues to be war torn, and where surrounding countries currently face significant political, social and economic difficulties.

It's a level of transformation that can be shocking. In 2010, I returned to the country for the first time in almost twenty years. When I left, there was literally nothing there. Not in the sense that someone in a developed Western country might say that a town or region has nothing in it; this wasn't a case of lacking a few luxuries, or perhaps being short on opportunities for youth. Instead, there were no real hospitals. There was no airport. There weren't hotels or universities. There were very few schools. Most of the houses consisted at least as much of earth as of modern building materials. There weren't even good roads. All that had been destroyed. That's how little there was when I left.

When I came back, that had changed so much it almost didn't seem like the same place. Areas that had been literally nothing but desert were now thriving with multiple construction projects. There were two major airports in Erbil and Sulaymaniyah, and a third being started in Dohuk so that suddenly I wasn't faced with a dangerous, hour's long drive to get into the country. There seemed to be private universities everywhere I looked, with people so eager to do well that they've driven a boom in demand for higher education. Even abroad, you now find Kurdish students succeeding in universities in all corners of the globe.

I saw a group of children on their way to school, wearing identically neat, perfect uniforms. That probably doesn't sound like much, but when I was a boy, I had to make do with clothes that my mother had patched up repeatedly, wearing them until they were either worn through so completely that not even she could repair them, or until I outgrew them. Now, here there were kids whose parents probably bought them a new uniform every time they found a way to tear or damage theirs.

I actually found myself feeling a little jealous of those kids. I started asking why I couldn't have been born twenty years later, so that I could have grown up in this new Kurdistan, enjoying the kind of opportunities that they will hopefully grow up thinking of as normal. If they work hard, these kids will have all the education and opportunities they need to become doctors, lawyers, or whatever else they want. They probably won't go hungry. They probably won't find themselves at serious risk of harm. They will probably have a chance at a real childhood before they have to be adults.

That is the way things should be, and I'm happy to say that it is the way things are these days in Kurdistan. It's the kind of place where children can grow up as children, then have some real opportunities as adults. In some ways, that's the best thing you can ask of a region. Yes, there is still significant ground to be made up in some areas, such as the number of children still pushed into work by poverty, but even on those issues, the numbers have fallen dramatically in just the last few years, so that while some seven percent of Iraqi children work overall, that figure is closer to two percent for Kurdistan.

Just as importantly, Kurdistan is a place that people are proud of now. When I first went back there, my family were only too ready to drive me around and show me how much things had changed. I think they enjoyed seeing my face every time we came across something that would have been inconceivable when I left, because it meant that someone was appreciating just how far Kurdistan had come. Although it might have had something to do with just how shocked I was by the extent of some of the changes, too.

Yet it does seem to be the case in general that people in Iraqi Kurdistan are proud of the direction that their region has gone in. They want people to notice the changes. They take the same pride in a new school or area of housing that they would have if they'd had something to do with building it directly. It's a place, not just where people have a kind of general civic pride, but where they have really bought into the idea of a region (a country in all but name) where things are advancing at a rapid rate. The claim to be a 'second Dubai' isn't just a boast about the level of success and wealth there in some quarters. It's a kind of goal; a clear vision of the future that they want for themselves and for Kurdistan. I'd like to think that I've made a lot out of myself, despite what Saddam's regime tried to do to me, and I intend to continue doing so. Well, Kurdistan is a whole region with the same feeling.

What kinds of changes have there been in Kurdistan in the last decade or so? (I may have left in 1993, but the truth is that the biggest changes only took place after the end of the civil war there in the late nineties, making Kurdistan's transformation all the more remarkable).

The most visible change comes in the form of rebuilding work. Whole villages and towns have been substantially rebuilt. In aerial photographs of cities such as Erbil, what is striking is not just the number of modern rows of apartment blocks and houses, but the fact that those areas not already rebuilt show signs of preparations for building work.

This rebuilding has often taken the form of major infrastructure projects. There are more hospitals now in the region than there ever were before, as well as a substantially increased number of schools, now teaching in Kurdish rather than the Arabic imposed from Bagdad. I have already mentioned probably the most impressive elements of this infrastructure, which come in the form of Kurdistan's major new airports. Erbil International Airport is particularly impressive, taking the site of an old military airbase and turning it into an important connection to the outside world from December

2003. By 2009, more than three hundred and fifty thousand people were coming through it per year[1].

As someone who now lives in the UK, I can't help contrasting that with the difficulties that arise every time there's a suggestion that one of the UK's airports should be developed. In this country, there are major political rows over the redevelopment of Heathrow, the country's biggest airport, along with consultation processes that look set to drag on for years. In Kurdistan, the construction of Erbil International Airport, from nothing to its first flights, took less than a year. There has also been significant investment in other aspects of infrastructure, from roads to more modern elements such as the provision of effective communications and ICT infrastructure.

These are the most visible elements, but there have also been major changes in other areas of life in the region. Economically, Kurdistan has boomed, growing in a way that many other regions around the globe, let alone within Iraq, can claim. With the infrastructure in place to exploit its vast natural resources, it is a region in a position to help secure the world's oil supply with the first new drilling concessions in Iraq for many years. Better than that, because Kurdistan has enough food to feed its population, the

---

1   http://www.erbilairport.net/

money from these additional resources is able to go on projects to keep the region moving forward.

Socially, there have been changes too. Women play a much fuller role in public life, and have greater access to basic freedoms, than in many areas of Iraq and surrounding countries. Kurdistan has female police officers and politicians, while women are freer to act as they wish there than in the vast majority of those countries around Kurdistan. I would never claim that things are perfect there, but in things such as the ban on Female Genital Mutilation in 2011, and in continuing efforts against violence towards women, I would at least like to suggest that it is a region where attempts are being made to secure the basic rights of its female population in a way that isn't always true of other places.

There are other areas in which Kurdistan seems to be socially ahead of many of its neighbours. The level of religious toleration in the region has been noted on several occasions, with Kurdistan's populations of Coptic Christians and followers of Yezidism able to live without the threats of violence that they might face just the other side of the border in Iran. Kurdistan is also home to numerous ethnic groups in addition to the Kurds, including Assyrians, Roma, and more. While there have been accusations of bias towards Kurdish interests in the region, it's also true that the Assyrians and other groups get specific representation in the regional government, and benefit from all the advantages of a region that is largely safe. If there's one group of people who don't want to persecute anyone, it's the Kurds.

Some of this might not sound perfect yet. I'd argue that very few places are perfect. I'd also argue that Kurdistan at least understands the direction in which it needs to go, and is taking active steps to get there. More than that, it is further along the road it needs to travel than almost any place has a right to be in just over a decade. It has gone from almost nothing to being one of the few safe regions in a war torn country, with a promising economic future and a present that is enough to make me stare at it in shock every time I go back there.

I'll be going into greater detail about the rebuilding process later, but there are many factors that have contributed to the speed and completeness of Kurdistan's rebuilding. Part of it is simply the place where it began, because in some ways it is easier to produce something from nothing than it is to change things that are already in existence.

A far more important factor comes in the form of the natural wealth, particularly in oil. Whatever you think of the role of oil in the Iraq war, we live in a world where there is a clear demand for the oil that Kurdistan is able to produce. Oil provides the money needed for the rebuilding process, even though it may also create some of the biggest challenges for the region in the future.

There's stability, too. It may seem like an obvious point, but it is easier to rebuild in a region where the threat of violence has been reduced than in one that continues to be dangerous. Because the three main areas of Iraqi Kurdistan were some of the first to be declared stable in the wake of the Iraq wars, they have actually been in a better position to start a process of recovery than many of those around them. That has given Kurdistan an opportunity to attract investment, as well as attracting talented, innovative people from all round Iraq, who want to live in a region where they feel safe and are able to contribute to Kurdistan as an on-going project.

Then there's the influence of the civil war. While Kurdistan is stable now, for years it was plagued by a vicious civil war where families couldn't trust their own members, while factions fought over the future political shape of the region. It meant that for a long time, the rebuilding process couldn't start, but once Kurdistan achieved relative stability, memories of the civil war may actually have helped to spur on successive governments in their efforts to improve the region.

All of these are important points, and ones I'll look at further, but for me, the most important element has been the pride I talked about before. It's the same pride that my family showed in taking me to see the new developments. It's the kind of pride that I see there even in strangers, who take great delight in pointing out how much things have changed when they realise that I don't normally live in Kurdistan.

It is, in a way, a kind of pride that comes out in impatience when things are wrong. Kurdistan has spent so long with things being bad that now; people aren't prepared to *wait* for things to be good. Instead, they want to go out and *make* it happen. They want things to be better right away. They don't want anywhere else to be a better place to live. It's a level of aspiration that isn't usually seen in a region, but when it is, it can utterly transform it.

It may seem at this point that I've been putting a lot of emphasis on the rebuilding process, as well as on how positive things are looking in Kurdistan. It may even seem a little unrealistic to focus on those aspects of a region that has been war torn in the past, and which has been the site of mass murder on an almost incomprehensible scale.

Yet I wanted to start this book by making one thing clear: Kurdistan is not a region that wants pity. The same pride that has pushed it to rebuild at a speed almost nowhere else could manage means that its people don't want to be seen as they tend to be seen on those rare occasions when the world remembers them, simply as the victims of Saddam Hussein's violence. That would be like viewing Jews purely in terms of the Holocaust, or the inhabitants of the various Balkan states only in terms of the atrocities of Pristina, or attacks on UN safe zones.

Kurdistan does not want pity, but it *does* deserve greater understanding and acceptance. It deserves an acknowledgement of the sheer scale of what it has achieved in the last decade and a half, because it achieved it in the wake of decades of officially sanctioned neglect and abuse, culminating in a campaign of violence that was essentially genocidal in nature. The region's achievements in rebuilding only become more impressive when you consider the impact of that campaign, and the sustained, systematic destruction that it brought about.

People deserve to know about that. They need to understand, not so that they can pity the region, but simply because it helps to explain so much of the way Kurdistan has tried to improve itself afterwards. They need to understand to stop it from ever happening again. They need to understand, because it is unacceptable that a genocide that was essentially ignored by many countries around the world at the time should continue to be ignored by history.

That sounds like it should be impossible, yet even my current home country, the UK, only recently officially recognized Saddam's attempts to eliminate the Kurds as genocide. This is a country that prides itself on a strong connection to history, yet this is one element that for a long time it seemed determined to forget. People I meet outside Kurdistan, meanwhile, often have little or no idea that many of the worst atrocities even happened. At best, they have a vague idea that Saddam hated the Kurds and employed chemical weapons against them, but just as often Kurdistan is confused with Kuwait, and people certainly don't understand the details of Halabja, the Anfal campaign, or their precursors. Even the justifications for Western intervention in Iraq focussed less on the murderous humanitarian abuses of the regime than on vague concerns about WMDs that could threaten their own countries.

Part of what I'm hoping to achieve with this book is much wider recognition for everything that happened to my people under Saddam's regime. I hope that if enough people understand what happened and why, it will help to prevent such a terrible thing from happening again. It might also be the case that sufficient public recognition of the genocide will eventually help to alter official positions on it, so that it is recognised by more than just a small number of institutions worldwide. Finally, I hope that by providing information on the way Kurdistan has rebuilt itself after these events, I can help to promote the region that has given me so much, and perhaps even help to make the case for its recognition as a country.

I also hope that I can help to fill in some of the gaps in the available literature on the genocidal campaigns against the Kurds. It seems like it should be a topic that attracts considerable attention, given the seriousness of the events involved. Yet in practice, there has been relatively little produced on it. Where there are other massacres and genocides that have produced whole miniature publishing industries, those perpetrated against the Kurds have resulted in a handful of books at best.

Some of those are very good. Michael J. Kelly[2] provides excellent information on what is usually seen as the key atrocity of Saddam's time in office, Halabja, while several other works, such as Susan Schuurman's *An 'Inconvenient' Atrocity*[3], also focus on it. Lawrence and Bird[4]

2   Michael J. Kelly, *Ghosts of Halabja* (Praeger Security International, 2008)
3   S. Schuurman, *An Inconvenient Atrocity* (MA thesis, University of New Mexico, 2007)
4   Q. Lawrence, *Invisible Nation,* (Walker and Company, New York, 2008), C. Bird,

have focussed more on Kurdistan in the after-math, providing an outsider's view of the rebuilding.

There are two main dangers here. The first is that we can end up seeing Halabja as the only event worth mentioning in the course of a whole campaign of genocide. By focussing on it to the exclusion of all else, we can even be left with the impression that there *was* no genocide, just a single gas attack. Hiltermann, for example, seems to view the rest of the Anfal as just the setting for Halabja, while many other writers do not see the Anfal as a continuation of the regime's previous policies. Instead, I would like to argue that Halabja and even the Anfal can only be properly seen in the context of an on-going process aimed first at the contain-ment and then the elimination of all Kurds, and particularly those from the Barzani tribe.

The second potential danger comes from being an outsider looking in, and is to some extent unavoidable. There is the academic tone of some works. Schuurman's work, for example, is actually a published version of her MA thesis, although it should be noted that she makes a significant effort to use individual accounts. Several of the other sources for information on the atrocities in Kurdistan come from published

A Thousand Sighs A Thousand Revolts, (Random House, New York, 2005)

reports by bodies such as Human Rights Watch. These represent great sources for understanding the bare historical bones of what was done and when. Perhaps even some of why. What they do not do, however, is to provide the feel of what occurred. Even though they do use individual accounts, they do not always fully understand what it was like to be there, because the authors were not there.

Indeed, in cases such as Hiltermann's *A Poisonous Affair*[5], it seems to me almost as though they do the opposite. In striving for the historical values of objective analysis and clarity, in stepping back far enough to provide the relevant statistics to damn Saddam, they also, almost inevitably, push the reader further away from the emotional reality of what was done. The saying goes that one death is a tragedy, while a million is a statistic. There's a possibility that by emphasising the statistical scale of this tragedy, otherwise wonderful books have achieved exactly that effect.

What can I do to avoid that? Clearly, I cannot ignore the scale of what has happened. Nor can I ignore facts and statistics where they are appropriate. I am not aiming for an academic text here though, not least because there are certainly other people out there who could

---

5   J.R. Hiltermann, *A Poisonous Affair*, (Cambridge, 2007)

do it better. Instead, I am hoping that by drawing on my personal experience of life in Kurdistan from 1974-1991, I will be able to add a personal, individual, element to the story of what happened. I do that here not because I believe my story to be any more important than those of the many, many people who died, but simply in the hope that adding my personal recollections to a broader account will make it easier for people to connect to the reality of what occurred.

Having said that, I would like to consider one more danger in this kind of endeavour; one that I believe has affected a number of books that touch on this area. There is a real danger, particularly in books in English, that the focus of the book becomes Saddam Hussein. Certainly, many books that touch on Halabja are actually biographies of Iraq's former dictator, or histories that focus almost entirely on what he did and when.

I believe that there are a number of reasons why this is generally the case. One is simply responsibility. Although it was not what he was tried and executed for, it is clear that Saddam gave the orders that led to the genocide against the Kurds. There is perhaps a feeling that any book about these atrocities must inevitably be about their author. I would disagree with that. While I fully intend to mention Saddam where necessary, I feel that focussing on him places attention on the decision making process, rather than on what happened on the ground.

Another reason, I suspect, is the ease of gathering information. Records from Saddam's trial provide us with a lot, while other records relating to events tend to link back to him too. It is entirely reasonable to expect that any book following the trail of records would include a considerable amount on him. It is also reasonable to expect that individuals with a general interest in the Iraq wars would focus on him, rather than on the effects of his genocidal campaigns.

There is also a slightly more worrying question of interest. The simple fact seems to be that books about Saddam Hussein sell better than those about events in Iraq many people have not heard of, and which are in any case on topics they may feel do not affect them directly. Genocide is not, when all is said and done, a topic that everyone wishes to read about, even though I believe it to be necessary if we are to avoid something similar happening again.

Those factors combine to produce a widespread focus on Saddam rather than my people. I want to say here and now that this is not a book about Saddam Hussein. He will be included where necessary, because it would be ludicrous not to mention the author of these atrocities in connection with them. However, my focus here will be on Kurdistan, and on the experience of being caught up in the events as they unfolded, rather than on a figure who was, while hated, also largely distant.

To make this book about Saddam would be to tell a far different story than the one I want to tell here. It would be a story set in Bagdad and internationally, when the heart of *this* story took place in Kurdistan. The evil of the men who made decisions that cost thousands of people their lives matters. Of course it matters. But what matters more here is understanding exactly what happened to the people of Kurdistan, as well as seeing some of the strength that they displayed in the face of it. This is a book about them, rather than Saddam Hussein, and I believe that is the only way it should really be.

It is a book about me too, of course, and I'm sure there are those who will think it is arrogant of me to put my experiences down like this when talking about events that involved so many people. Please understand, I am in no way claiming that I was at the heart of these events. I was young when many of them occurred, indeed on at least one occasion it was the fact that I was so young that saved my life.

Yet as I have outlined above, I believe that it is my ability to add my personal experiences to the history of what happened that will help to make this history of what happened in Kurdistan real for you. That is why I have included my memories. It is also why I have included a number of personal opinions on the factors behind particular events. I am not claiming that my personal opinion constitutes historical truth. Nor am I claiming to be in possession of facts about Kurdistan that other people do not have. I am simply presenting my view of what happened and while I hope my opinions make sense to you, I mostly hope that they will help you to see how events looked to those of us caught up in them.

That means, inevitably, that the structure of this book will be a little unusual. My personal experiences will be caught up with more general observations on historical events, and with my opinions on the ways those events came into being. In several instances, I have taken the time to explore what I believed to have been the case even when later evidence has shown something else to be true. In that way, I hope to ground the information here in my experience, and also to demonstrate the differences between what the evidence suggests and what appeared to be true at the time. I will, of course, try to be clear about what is my opinion and experience, and what is established fact.

So, how do I intend to go about explaining the whole of the genocide against the Kurds? I

plan to start by explaining what I feel is necessary background. Those who know the region
may not find that necessary, but it is my hope
to bring this genocide to the attention of those
who do *not* have an existing stake in Kurdistan,
so I hope that you will bear with me if you are
familiar with it. It is also necessary if we are to
understand the context of the violence.

Then, I will explore the displacement of the
Kurds and my own experiences of being put
into one of the camps built to contain us. I will
explore life in the camps, and what it was like
day to day to live knowing that the government
hated us. I will look at the taking of more than
eight thousand men and boys from the camps,
and their probable fate. I will do this partly
because these events deserve never to be forgotten, but also to show that they were connected
to the process and thinking that produced the
Anfal.

I will, of course, examine what happened at
Halabja. It is impossible not to, but I will also
explore the impact of the wider Anfal campaign,
as well as looking at what it meant for those of
us already trapped by the regime. I will explore
what we knew about it, what it meant for us
from day to day, and the fears that came along
with it.

I hope to show that the Anfal mirrored some
of the wider tactics used previously, that it was

a genocide, and that the regime's propaganda misled popular understanding of what was going on.

Because this is a book about Kurdistan, however, I will also explore the way the hardest times ended. I will look at my people's escape from captivity, at the civil war that followed, and at the efforts that have occurred since to rebuild the region. Kurdistan's history is about so much more than just what was done to it, after all.

Yet there are hard questions that need to be asked, and I plan to ask them here. Why has what happened to my people not been fully recognised as genocide in all countries, when it fits in with the pattern of genocides the world over? Why have some countries, such as the UK, waited so long to recognise it as such? Why was it allowed to happen by individuals within Iraq, by Iraq's neighbours, and by the international community? Could it ever happen again in Kurdistan, and what does the future hold for the region?

This is a lot to attempt to answer in a relatively short space, and in some ways this is a complex book. It is my story and my people's story rolled into one. Yet I continue to believe that is essential. Because if, as the saying insists, a million deaths is just a statistic, one life will have to make you see more than that. If there is one thing I hope that you will understand, having read this book, it is simply that every life taken in Kurdistan was that of a human being, probably loved, certainly missed. Yet despite it all, Kurdistan has still rebuilt.

How many places can say that?

1

Kurdistan – a brief history

Fully understanding what has happened in Kurdistan in recent times requires a certain amount of knowledge of both the history and geography of the region. Understanding my connections to some of the events that I will describe later in this book, as well as my attitudes to them, requires an understanding of the connections my family has to the region and to the events that have shaped its history. In this chapter, I will attempt to provide all three of those elements.

Geographically, Kurdistan is complex, simply because it has yet to be recognised as an official country by the UN or anyone else. There are Kurds living in regions of a number of countries, including Iraq, Iran, Syria and Turkey. There are other communities of Kurds living in countries throughout the world, particularly in areas of the former USSR such as Armenia, but the four countries I have just mentioned are the most prominent ones, both in terms of numbers, and because of the way their Kurdish populations fit together.

What I mean by that is that Kurds are not

spread evenly throughout those countries, except where they have been forced to do so by their governments. Instead, there are distinctly Kurdish areas of each that fit together like pieces of a jigsaw to produce a large extra-national 'region' of Kurdistan. It is a region that includes much of the north of Iraq, along with parts of eastern Turkey, north-eastern Syria, western Iran, and the extreme south of Armenia.

It has been estimated that these regions contain approximately forty million Kurds, the majority of whom are resident in Turkey. That is a huge figure. It is equal, for example to approximately forty percent of the UK's population, and is larger than the populations of countries such as the Netherlands, Yemen, and Ghana. Crucially, it is also larger than the population of Syria alone (at around twenty-two million). It is also enough to make Kurds the third largest ethnic group in the Middle East. These numbers also lead the Kurds, and many of those talking about them, to call them the largest ethnic group without a nation in the world.

It is necessary to understand this to fully grasp the history of the Kurds, as we will see later in this chapter. For our purposes, however, when I refer to Kurdistan, I will usually be referring specifically to *Iraqi* Kurdistan. When I am not, I will try to make that clear. Kurdistan in this sense refers to a much smaller region, taking in only a band running across the northern borders of Iraq, the precise extent of which is currently a matter of dispute with the Iraqi government, particularly over the city of Kirkuk.

This usage of 'Kurdistan' to mean 'Iraqi Kurdistan' is a common one both in the region and beyond these days. It has a lot to do with how far the region has come in achieving a degree of autonomy and independence. It is, quite simply, the most readily identifiable and official unit of territory available to which to apply the name. It is also in some ways a political point. Individuals inside Kurdistan are sometimes quite careful not to use the term to apply to the wider region, especially when making the case for Kurdistan to be recognised as a country. This is because they know the hostility that seeming to make a claim to the whole region as part of an independent country would provoke. Several of the powers immediately surrounding Kurdistan, as we will see, are still largely hostile to the idea of a Kurdish homeland.

I will be mostly limiting my comments here to Iraqi Kurdistan because that is the area of my experience. That is where I grew up. That is where I was while Saddam and his party tried to kill us, and that is where I have watched the rebuilding, taking pride in the extent to which my people have made this small band of land so much more than it was. It is also the region in which the genocide occurred.

The band of territory that comprises Kurdistan today is approximately consistent with the northern no-fly zone imposed over Northern Iraq by the US from 1992 While I will argue that the current situation of Kurdistan is largely down to the efforts of its inhabitants, there can be no denying that the prevention of airborne assaults on Kurdistan's towns helped to provide it with time in which to stabilise and grow. More than that, it is easy to contrast the areas that fell within the no-fly zone with those outside it, and the continuing instability in some of them. At the same time though, I wish to make it clear that Kurdistan is not solely down to the existence of the no-fly zone. After all, those areas covered by the equivalent zone in the south have not developed in the same ways.

Politically, this area consists of three distinct governmental districts, centred on the cities of Erbil, Dohuk and Sulaymaniyah. These are the three most important cities of Kurdistan, with Erbil (sometimes spelled Arbil, and occasionally known by the older name of Hawler) forming the overall regional capital. These divisions are old ones, linked in part to those used under the Persian and Ottoman empires, though today they continue to exist primarily because of the administrative efficiency they offer. They also continue to exist partly because of differences in political influence between them, which came out most starkly in the late nineteen nineties when they came under the control of competing political parties and fighting ensued. Although this violence is now over, some of the political divisions remain in the differing characters of the regions, and the influence of Kurdistan's political parties still varies with those regions.

The important point to note for now, however, is the extent to which entire regions in Kurdistan are bound up with their key cities. If someone says Erbil, Dohuk or Sulaymaniyah, they might mean the city or the region around that city. And it probably wouldn't make too much difference which they meant, because anything connected to the wider region would almost automatically be connected to the city too. Kurdistan is a region whose cities are crucial to an even greater extent than they are in the majority of other places.

The current reasons for that urban focus are numerous. The ability for cities to provide an identifiable focus for investment and growth is one. Whether with NGOs or private companies, it is generally easier for people to focus money in the cities and let benefits flow outward from them than it is to attempt to invest directly in more rural areas. There is also a question of demographics to consider. Currently, more than ninety percent of Kurdistan's population is resident in urban areas. Failing to consider its cities, therefore, would be to fail to consider the vast majority of Kurdistan's population.

The reason for that urbanised population, and another reason why the cities are so important, is the extent to which the rural population of Kurdistan was eliminated or removed by Saddam's troops. In the nineteen sixties and before, it seems likely that Kurdistan's population was much more rural than it is today, even if we lack the census figures to prove it one way or another. We certainly know that increased urbanisation has been a side effect of some of the events described here, with the result that those events continue to have knock on effects on the way in which Kurdistan functions.

In terms of physical geography, Kurdistan is a varied land. The image of Iraq generally is of a desert nation, yet even that is a distortion. Not everywhere in the country is desert. There are areas of grasslands and wetlands, even swamps. Kurdistan is every bit as diverse. There are dry desert areas, certainly, but there are also rivers and lakes, forests and fertile valleys. It is those that have made an essentially agrarian lifestyle possible for large swathes of Kurdistan's history. They have also helped to ensure that the region has been able to support its people, even in times of great hardship. More recently, those geographical conditions have helped to provide Kurdistan with food security, allowing it to be a net exporter of basic foodstuffs.

I touched on this in the introduction, but Kurdistan is also a region rich in natural resources. Oil is a particularly important one. Although the scale of oil production from Kurdistan isn't currently at the level of Iraq's southern oilfields, for example, forecasts still say that by the end of 2012 it will still stand at an impressive 500,000 barrels per day and is set to rise further.[6] In recent times, those natural resources have helped to provide Kurdistan with the finances needed to improve itself. We will see when we look at the region's history, however, that those resources have also made it, on many occasions, too precious to other countries for them to allow it independence.

Before we get to that, however, I would like to discuss arguably the most important geographical feature of Kurdistan: its mountains. Large portions of Kurdistan, particularly on the border with Iran, are mountainous. The region includes mountains such as Judi, Ararat and Zagros, along with numerous other peaks and smaller hills. Mountains are crucial to the Kurdish way

6   http://www.krg.org/uploads/documents/03_Table_Production_and_Revenue_Forecasts.pdf

of life. Kurdish folklore is largely focussed on the mountains, while key sayings such as 'the Kurds have no friends but the mountains' stress their importance in helping my people survive and thrive through the centuries. Indeed, I think it is reasonable to say that without the mountains, my people would not exist as a separate people. They certainly wouldn't have many of the attitudes to life that they do.

Why do I say this? What do mountains mean? This is a theme explored more fully by Bird[7] but in general, they mean two things: isolation and protection. Isolation is simple. In mountainous regions, people and communities throughout history have found it hard to reach even near neighbours. They certainly haven't been in a position to travel to distant capitals, or to do business with the rest of a widely spread out country.

They have, instead, been largely separated from anything beyond the mountains, forced to be self-reliant and to place a strong emphasis on local identities, even to the exclusion of national identities that people sitting in cities on the plains might wish them to have. For this reason, mountainous regions frequently produce some of the strongest separate regional identities, as well as some of the strongest calls for separate governance in those countries where they sit.

_____

7   For example at Bird, p14

They feel no sense of connection to the rest of a supposed country, for the simple reason that frequently, they are *not* connected to it, thanks to the separations imposed by the mountains. That is probably less true in this age of instant communications and rapid transport, but even with them, mountains create a feeling of separation.

They also provide protection. Throughout history, people who have been persecuted or driven out of other lands have headed for more mountainous regions, where large armies cannot march in formation, where it is possible to slip away from would be attackers before they can get to you, and where settlements can be defended by the natural protections of slopes and bottleneck valleys. That is as true of Kurdistan as anywhere else, thanks to neighbours who have repeatedly sought to attack my people, and even destroy the idea of them (as the Turks did for much of the twentieth century when they officially insisted that the Kurds did not exist, but were merely Turks who lived in the mountains and who chose not to use their 'real' language).

The protection of the mountains has literally meant the survival of my people on several occasions, including during Saddam's attempts at genocide. Throughout the fight against Saddam, the mountains provided protection for the peshmerga, those men who fought for Kurdistan's freedom. They also provided numerous pathways back and forth between Iran and Iraq, allowing avenues of escape for those people able and willing to run.

The protection of the mountains has also worked in a subtler way in Kurdistan, by providing a unifying element across national borders. Their presence has provided a defined Kurdish region and protected that region from official attempts to legislate it out of existence. They have made it hard for outside administrators to come in and expect to simply reorganise everything, with the result that the three provinces that now make up Kurdistan retained their shape despite the attempts to destroy the Kurdish people.

I have used the term 'Kurdish people' several times now. What exactly does that mean? Clearly, I am not just referring to the inhabitants of the region, because it would be perfectly possible for an Arab to live in Kurdistan or for a Kurd to live almost anywhere in the world, the way I live in the UK. Indeed, many of the inhabitants of Kurdistan are non-Kurdish, and one of the strengths of the region as it grows comes in the form of the increasing efforts it is making to recognise and accommodate all sections of society.

In that sense, to be from Kurdistan does not

necessarily mean to be a member of a particular ethnic group, yet to be Kurdish is a different matter. There is a clear Kurdish ethnicity that transcends borders. It is part of what makes the movement towards the creation of a Kurdish homeland so important.

Yet to be Kurdish is not all one thing. Because the Kurds have historically been tribal, family and tribal affiliations are important, even in the modern region. The symbols of those affiliations continue to be worn by my people. I, for example, am Barzani. The Barzani are readily identifiable in Kurdistan through the red and white headscarves they wear, with family members wearing two, one on top of the other. There are many other tribes, but the Barzani are important because of the roles their members have played in many of Kurdistan's attempts to achieve independence, and in the rebuilding process after the fall of Saddam.

There are also linguistic differences. Kurdish is a complex language, with numerous dialects. The three most important dialect groups are Kurmanji (or Northern Kurdish) Sorani (or Central Kurdish) and those dialects spoken by Southern Kurds. The principal dialect for Kurds generally is Kurmanji, with around eight to ten million speakers, but when we are talking about Iraqi Kurdistan generally, Sorani is more important, being spoken as the main dialect in both Erbil and Sulaymaniyah. Kurmanji is important in Dohuk, but it is a less vital city for the administration of the region, and in any case, there is a certain amount of overlap between regions, with speakers of each dialect present in both areas.

You might be wondering at this point about the claims of Kurds to be a single group if they do not speak one language. Some people will almost certainly be wondering about whether Kurdistan can function as the nation many people want it to be if those within it are not all capable of understanding one another. I feel it is important to address those points here. First, it is important to remember that these are not separate languages. They are dialects of the same language, close enough that speakers of one will often understand speakers of another. Second, many Kurds will speak more than one of these dialects, along with other languages. Thirdly, the experiences of some of the largest countries in the world, such as India and China, show that areas supporting a wide range of dialects and languages can still function as coherent administrative and cultural units.

Religiously, Kurdistan is primarily Sunni Muslim. There are also Kurds who are Shi'ite, but in Iraq, their numbers are somewhat less than they are in Iran or Turkey. Kurdistan is relatively religiously open, tolerating a wide variety of religious views, including groups with links to the region's more ancient religious beliefs such as Zoroastrianism or Yezidism. Although there have been religious tensions in the region, generally, those are much less pronounced than they are in many of the surrounding countries. Certainly, there are a greater number of religious freedoms in the democratic environment of Kurdistan than there are in countries that do not run as openly.

Kurdistan's history is not generally well known by those outside it, and in many ways this is unfortunate, because it is only by understanding the history of the region that we are in a position to place some of the things that have happened there in their proper context. While this overview of Kurdistan's history is necessarily both brief and focussed on more recent events, it is important to understand that both Kurdistan and Kurdish identity reach deep into the past.

It seems likely, from those archaeological estimates that are available, that Kurdistan was one of the earliest areas to adopt agriculture as a way of life. We also know that the ancient civilisations of Mesopotamia (Babylonian, Assyrian, Sumerian), whose territories included parts of where Kurdistan stands now, were some of the most advanced of their time, contributing significant advances to the world in such areas as writing, the recording of time, mathematics and more. Archaeological investigations in Erbil, formerly known as Hawler, show that it is one of the oldest continuously occupied sites on the planet, with inhabitants from at least 4000 BC on.

Of course, in saying that, we must recognise that the early Mesopotamian civilisations were not Kurdish ones as we know them. Yet the Kurds did quickly come into being as a separate, defined people. Bird[8] argues convincingly that the idea of Kurdish identity was present even as early as 401 BC, with 'Karduchoi' who were probably Kurds, mentioned by the Greek, Xenophon as Greeks fought against the Persians. By that time, we also know that areas of what is now Kurdistan had been under Persian control for more than two hundred years, after conquering them from the Babylonians.

The control of Kurdistan by the Persians probably helped to create some of the general divisions by which the region is governed even now. The Persians governed through a system of caliphates that, while not exactly mirroring the three regions into which Kurdistan is divided today, did at least feature cities such as Erbil as primary power centres.

Probably the most significant historical change in the region was the introduction of Islam from

---

8   *Ibid.* p10

637 onwards. Not only did it serve to redefine the religious identity of the entire region, it also helped to redefine its ethnic makeup, by bringing in Arab settlers, often in dominant positions over Kurdish subjects. Despite this, in this period, it is likely that Kurdistan had a great deal of autonomy, with four Kurdish princes ruling over separate regions in the wider area. Some Kurds had the opportunity to achieve even more than that, with arguably the most famous of all Kurdish rulers, Saladin, achieving rulership of much of the surrounding region, as well as significant military victories over invading forces during the third crusade.

From there until approximately 1500, Kurdistan was again split into a number of separate principalities, each broadly autonomous from day to day but still owing an overall fealty to the Persian Empire. At that point, things started to change, with the various principalities of Kurdistan being targets for the expansion of the Ottoman Empire. Kurdish princes were able to negotiate for the retention of their rights and privileges when the Ottomans took their lands, but only in exchange for guarding the borders of the empire. This was, it should be pointed out, not a quick process. The last independent Kurdish principality did not fall until the middle of the nineteenth century, when much of Kurdistan was already experiencing significant problems with plague, and many of the inhabitants were forced to take up a more nomadic lifestyle to survive. This period, although seemingly chaotic, was of key importance in reinforcing the tribal bonds that still have such a role in the region today.

Kurdistan remained a part of the Ottoman Empire until the outbreak of World War One in 1914. During that terrible conflict, however, many inhabitants of the region agreed to side with the British and their allies, rising up in rebellion against the Ottomans. Today, it tends to be other theatres of that conflict that are most readily remembered, yet the conflict in the Middle East was just as crucial to the progress of the war as that in Western Europe, in many respects. The role played by the Kurds was crucial in preventing the might of the Ottoman Empire from fully contributing to other aspects of the conflict. The expectation among my people was that, as the already decaying Ottoman Empire collapsed in the wake of the war, they would achieve an independent homeland that would be self-governing. They already knew that was something the Turks would never give them if they did not act.

For a while, it looked like they might get everything they desired. Sheikh Mahmoud Barzani was appointed by the British to govern in 1918, and argued for an independent Kurdish homeland. The American president Woodrow Wilson, meanwhile, had announced that non-Turks formerly under Turkish rule should be allowed the opportunity for autonomous development in the twelfth of fourteen points he published in 1918.

The Treaty of Sevres, signed on the 10th of August 1920, seemed to guarantee that independence still further. Made between the temporary Kurdish government, the British and the French, it guaranteed that as soon as the League of Nations believed that they were capable of governing themselves, the Kurdish people would have independence. Looked at through today's eyes, the terminology of the treaty is more than a little patronizing, but that wasn't the major flaw with it. The main problem with the Treaty of Sevres was that it was never fully ratified.

Instead, it was quickly superseded by the 1923 Treaty of Lausanne. That is one treaty that it is hard for the Kurdish people to either forgive or forget. It set out rights for an extended Turkey, while allowing the Great Powers to hold inter-ests in portions of the Ottoman Empire's former holdings. Nowhere did it so much as mention the possibility of creating a homeland for the Kurds.

There are three probable reasons for that, which I feel are important, because they will probably resonate with some of the ways in which Saddam's later genocidal campaign was ignored. The first was the presence of Kurdistan's rich natural resources, and in particular its oil. Creating an independent Kurdish homeland would have potentially removed control of the production of that oil from Western powers. The second is the attitude hinted at in the Treaty of Sevres. The so called Great Powers of the time felt that they were better placed to make decisions about the future of the Kurdish people than the Kurds themselves. That attitude was reinforced by a visit from League of Nations inspectors, which recommended that Kurdistan as we know it today should be part of Iraq, with the British running the country for the next twenty five years to ensure the well-being of Kurds within it. It was the attitude of a parent deciding that a child wasn't ready to make decisions for themselves.

The third reason was the rise in Turkey of Mustafa Kemal Ataturk in Turkey. Although it would be naïve to ignore the other factors behind the refusal to create an independent Kurdistan, that was the immediate change of circumstances that persuaded the victorious powers to go back on their stated intentions. It is a pattern we see repeated through much of Kurdistan's history, with outside powers putting the immediate demands of realpolitik before promises made to the Kurdish people.

The result was the creation of Iraq, and the installation of King Faisal by the British. Sheik Mahmoud Barzani had begun a rebellion against British rule as early as 1919, suspending it only when he believed that Kurdistan might become independent, then resuming it when it became clear that nothing was going to change. There were further rebellions in Syria and Turkey, followed by arguably the most important such revolt of recent times, between 1943 and 1945.

That revolt was led by General Mullah Mustafa Barzani, whose son is currently the president of Kurdistan and who is one of the region's most important nationalist figures. He attempted, essentially, to repeat what his people managed in the First World War, using the dying days of a conflict to lever their people away from an empire in which they were trapped. When the revolt failed, General Mullah Mustafa Barzani was forced to flee to Iran, where he continued to pursue the nationalist cause until he was exiled to the USSR, taking three hundred followers with him. My uncle was one of those followers, travelling with him as they attempted to set up a homeland for Kurds within the soviet borders. For a time, it even succeeded, until the Mahabad Republic's soviet supporters pulled away from it, leaving the way clear for many of those involved to be killed.

This succession of rebellions makes it tempting to think of the Kurds as somehow inherently rebellious, or at least to see a unified pattern between them. In fact, the rebellions spanned five countries and almost thirty years. More than that, there is a danger in seeing them that way, especially when combined with the traditional view of the Kurds as a warlike mountain people. It is a combination that results in seeing them, not as a people labouring under broken promises and attacks from the outside, but as a problem to be solved. It is, in my opinion, at least partly the kind of thinking that led Saddam to attempt to wipe us out, and will be crucial to understanding the progress of the genocide later.

Before things could get to that point, of course, he still had to come to power. In Iraq, the monarchy fell in 1958. That sparked a particularly unsettled period for the country, including another revolt by General Mullah Mustafa Barzani's followers from 1961-1966. In 1968, the Ba'ath power rose to power following the fall of the military regime. Saddam was not in control of the Ba'ath party at that point, but he was still one of its most prominent members, and seems always to have been intended for its top position.

There was continuing rebellion from Kurdish peshmerga at that point, until in 1970, Saddam was sent north with the mission of making peace. It is a mission that does not sit well with what we know happened next, but may actually go some way to explaining Saddam's hatred of my people. Initially, the mission was hailed as a success, but fighting resumed the next year.

There was another attempt to forge peace in 1974, with an attempt to create a Kurdish Autonomous Region, but the discussions never seem to have progressed very far, thanks to arguments over Kirkuk. These are similar to the arguments that still occur today, but then, their consequences were much more severe, as we will see in the coming chapters.

1974 is the point I have picked to begin this story in earnest for two reasons. The first is that it seems to me to be the point at which any attempt to accommodate the Kurds was abandoned by the Iraqi government. The second is that it is the point at which my own experience begins to connect to the story of what happened, because 1974 was the year I was born, in the village of Sherwan, in the Barzan region.

2

The Seventies –
a prelude to genocide

It is strange sometimes how little focus there is on the events of the 1970s in books about Kurdistan. They are not ignored, exactly, but they are treated in many ways as being of lesser importance than Halabja and the Anfal. Perhaps that is because those two historical events are the ones that resulted in some of the most obvious and verifiable losses of life. Perhaps it is because the use of chemical weapons in Halabja is the story that people want to tell, with the result that even the much bloodier Anfal often takes second place. Perhaps it is because authors genuinely see those attempts at genocide as unconnected to the preceding fifteen years.

Certainly, that has been the overall impression I have gained, even if it was not the various authors' intention while writing. Halabja and the Anfal are treated in the major-ity of works, if not as something completely disconnected from the past, then certainly as something separate. The events of the 1970s are occasionally cited as part of the explanation for why those of 1987-8 occurred, but they are not generally treated as part of a wider campaign against the Kurds. The two periods are treated as being of essentially different qualities, with the 1970s forming a counter insurgency campaign, while 1987-8 was a more concerted attempt at destroying my people.

I am going to argue in this chapter and beyond that this view, while understandable, is flawed. That the Anfal, of which the Halabja bombing was a part, was a difference of degree rather than of intention. More than that, understanding the events of the late 1980s in isolation robs them of much of their force. They become a one off massacre, rather than a part of a continuing campaign aimed at eventual genocide. That is not acceptable. It is only by understanding the events of the 1970s, and seeing the connection to those later events, that we can see that the ultimate aim of Saddam and his party was the destruction of my people.

For the earliest years of this, my recollections are limited, as I was very young. Nevertheless, my family was involved in many of the events that took place in the 1970s, and they have been able to supply me with details of what happened to us. I will be using those memories in conjunction with my analysis of the history as I set it out here. Let us start by looking at the two attempts to broker peace with the Kurds, and with the Barzani tribe in particular, in the early 1970s. What were they for? What were the terms? Why did they fail? Just as importantly, can we reasonably say that there was ever an intention on the part of the Iraqi government to make them work?

There are two main agreements involved here. There is the one that was produced in 1970, brokered, almost ironically, by Saddam. The story goes that he went to Kurdistan, got a meeting with General Mullah Mustafa Barzani, put down several blank sheets of paper, and refused to leave until they hammered out a deal that would stop the Kurdish uprising in the north of the country. It is a story that was obviously designed to glorify Saddam within Iraq and boost his position within the country at a time when he was not yet even the de-facto ruler (he became head of the armed forces from 1976 and can be considered the most powerful man in the country from that point even if he did not become the official ruler until 1979).

At the same time though, it is a story with a lot to tell us. It tells us that as early as that point, Saddam was a man concerned with finding a solution to the 'problem' of the Kurds. That is an attitude that seems to carry through much of what follows. It also tells us that Saddam was very personally invested in the 1970 deal, putting a part of his personal reputation on the line to broker it. When the deal fell apart months afterwards, it is likely that he took it, not as a natural part of doing business in a complex and often fractious region, but as a personal betrayal.

At the close of this chapter, I will set out arguments for continuity of thinking regarding my people on Saddam's part. I will argue that either he and many of his supporters intended to destroy the Kurds all along, or that they consistently sought a solution to the 'problem' of Kurdish nationalism that became increasingly violent as time went on. Regardless of which argument you the reader come away feeling is the correct one, 1970 is a key moment.

So is 1974, because it is possible that, had a permanent deal been agreed then, events would have turned out very differently. Unfortunately, the 1974 agreement did not even make it to the status of a full agreement. It broke down in the middle of talks over a Kurdish Autonomous Region, because the Bagdad regime was unwilling to allow Kirkuk to be a part of it.

There were other problems. In my opinion, the failure of both agreements comes down to a combination of fundamental differences in what the Bagdad government and Kurdish leaders wanted, failures of trust and implementation, and the failure of an increasingly urbanised and centralised Bagdad regime to understand the implications of Kurdistan's rural, tribal past.

My people wanted what they have wanted for centuries, and what many of them still want: their own land, free from the control of governments run for the benefit of Arab or other populations to their exclusion. That desire has been clear and consistent for long enough that it is hard to see how the Bagdad government could not have understood it. Yet it is obvious that the Bagdad government did not, or at least, that it did not understand the depth of my people's commitment to the cause. Hearing those who fought speak, it is obvious that in 1974 in particular, they saw the conflict as almost a holy war on behalf of the cause of freedom.

That seems fundamentally incompatible with what Bagdad wanted. What that government wanted is probably what the majority of governments ultimately want: stability. In particular, having a revolt covering much of the north of their country hampered the Bagdad government's military stability in a period where hostilities with Iran were escalating.

In theory, therefore, an autonomous region was the perfect solution. The problem came in terms of other kinds of stability the Bagdad government wanted to maintain. There was territorial stability, or the basic unwillingness of any government to give away land that it regarded as its own. There was economic stability, or Bagdad's fundamental unwillingness to give up precious oil resources, particularly around Kirkuk. There was also a need for the maintenance of lines of authority, and control over the country's inhabitants. All of these needs meant that, while promising an independent area might have been the best solution militarily, actually delivering it in a sufficiently meaningful sense to meet Kurdish desires would have been impossible.

It is hardly surprising, therefore, that the Kurds, and the Barzani in particular, continued to revolt. The surprising thing is perhaps that my people were able to do so as successfully as they were, becoming far more than just a minor local revolt that could be easily put down. The reasons for that success are numerous, and include such things as the fighting spirit of the peshmerga fighters, the cover of the mountains, the strong history of support for such revolts, and the distance from Bagdad. However, the later failure of the revolt suggests that one factor was of key importance: outside backing.

Repeatedly in their history, my people have sought aid from stronger outside countries in standing up to their rulers. In 1973 (the attempts at a peace treaty came after the start of this more serious round of revolt), that aid came from Iran, backed by the United States.

The involvement of the USA was crucial. Many of my people have lived in Iran for years, and many more fled there in the course of the events I will describe here. In that sense, Iran has always been willing to provide the Kurds with a certain amount of assistance. Yet it has generally been quite *reluctant* assistance. We are not persecuted there the way we have been in Turkey, but there was always the impression of the Kurds being largely unwanted there. My people were more than aware thanks to numerous opportunities to find it out first hand, that assistance from Iran only came for as long as it was beneficial to Iran, and that it was primarily interested in destabilising Iraq, not in a united Kurdistan.

The involvement of the United States seemed to promise so much more for my people. Here was a country, after all, that had been founded on rebellion against distant rulers. A country that had basic freedoms enshrined at the heart of its constitution, and which had a vested interest in extending its influence in the region. Remember too that the closest my people had come to the creation of an independent state had been under the auspices of the world's other superpower, the USSR, with the brief experiment of the Republic of Mahabad. It may have seemed that the backing of the United States represented the best opportunity for my people to finally carve out the independent existence they wanted.

In that sense, the desire for the end result may have blinded them to some of the facts around them. Facts like the United States just coming to the end of a deeply unpopular and lengthy involvement in Vietnam. After such a costly and brutal war, it simply wasn't a country looking for involvement in another major military intervention at that point. It might have been looking to achieve a measure of destabilisation of Iraq, or even an excuse to become more closely involved diplomatically in the region, but it seems always to have been the case that the Kurds were to be used as proxies in a conflict only for a limited time. There certainly does not seem to have been the intention to help them create a fully independent state.

How limited was the support? The answer to that is simple. It lasted just long enough to bring Iraq and Iran together at the OPEC negotiating table in 1975. Saddam Hussein, in his then capacity as vice-chairman of the Revolution Command Council, was one of the negotiators, while the Shah of Iran was the other. On the 6th of May 1975, they agreed on the mid-point of the Shatt al-Arab river as the official border between Iran and Iraq.

They also agreed, fatally for so many of my people, that each would stop supplying weapons and support to Kurdish fighters within the other's borders.

That makes it sound like the extent of support was balanced, or even like there was a proxy war going on with Kurds on both sides killing one another in a senseless civil war. The way the agreement is phrased makes it sound almost as though Iran and Iraq were doing them a favour by stopping the violence. In fact, far more Kurds were engaged in violence against Iraq than Iran, and an agreement to cut off support to 'both' sides was actually an agreement to abandon those of my people left in Iraq to whatever fate the Iraqi regime decided for them. For what turned out to be only a five year cessation of war between Iran and Iraq, both Iran and the United States effectively condemned thousands of my people to death.

There is a famous phrase used by Henry Kissinger in relation to the Algiers Accord, which is that "covert action should not be confused with missionary work." It is essentially a defence of that abandonment, based on the idea that the USA's only obligation to Kurdistan was a moral one, and that morality had only a limited place in the reality of Cold War politics. It was the idea that the United States involved itself in the revolt to achieve particular objectives and to further its interests, so it should not have been a surprise that it walked away when further intervention would not have served those interests, no matter what the resulting damage.

It is, in short, an admission. It is an admission that Kissinger and others in the US government knew that there would be significant negative effects for my people after the accords. It is an admission that, knowing that, they still chose to walk away. It is, more than that, a bald statement of something my people have had to learn about international relations the hard way: that no matter who declares themselves your friend, they will ultimately act in the interests of their own country. As the saying goes, the only friends the Kurds have are the mountains.

In the mid-1970s, they quickly came to need the sanctuary of the mountains again. Almost as soon as the Algiers Accords were signed, it became clear that the Iraqi government intended to move military forces north in significant numbers. That may sound like I am crediting my people with greater foreknowledge of events than they in fact possessed, or attributing the status of knowledge to what were at the time merely fears on the basis that those fears came to pass.

Yet we must remember that there were Kurdish elements within the Iraqi army who were able to give those in Kurdistan a certain amount of information. Not much, and it was mixed in with rumour, but people definitely knew that something was coming.

How could they believe otherwise? Like everyone else, they could see that Saddam was a man trying to make his military reputation to cement his place in the country. They also knew that he was not a man to forgive anything that he saw as a betrayal. More than that, many of them had lived through the aftermath of previous revolts, and were familiar with the kinds of tactics that were typically employed by governments in their wake. There were many villages in Kurdistan that had been rebuilt several times in the preceding hundred years, when government forces under the British, the Iraqi kings, or the Ba'ath had razed them.

Perhaps that is one reason why so many stayed behind in the end. There was certainly a sense of reprisals coming, but my people have lived through so many attacks from Bagdad over the years that perhaps many of them felt that they would weather this storm the same way that they had weathered the ones in the past. Many Kurdish families elected to stay, even once it became clear that the peshmerga were no longer in a position to win the war in the immediate term.

Many more fled to Iran, in what has to be one of the largest known outpourings of refugees in Kurdistan's history. As many as a million of my people fled the country, with almost four hundred thousand fleeing to Iran. The group leaving for Iran included Mustafa Barzani, along with many of the most prominent members of the Barzani tribe.

I write "largest known" above, because it is only in modern times that we have been able to put numbers on such large scale displacements of people. It is, after all, only through the rise of more centralised governments that borders have become so clearly marked and defined. In many ways, while it is obviously good that so many of my people were able to escape what came next by getting to the right side of the Iran-Iraq border, I have to wonder if those clear lines are always a good thing.

Traditionally, my people have been able to wander across the whole region of the mountains, as their distribution across many countries shows. They were able to escape threats, take their way of life with them, and then return once the threat had receded. In the 1970s, however, crossing a border to escape a threat made them refugees, unable to go on with their lives until the Iranian government said they could.

I know from those who went that it was a long process. Iran was not happy to have so many people arriving across its borders, even if those same people had been fighting its war with Iraq just a little while before. Many of my people found themselves pushed into refugee camps and then spread out across Iran, in ways that meant they were often cut off from the communities and families they knew. Whether that was simply a case of Iran putting administrative ease before the well-being of those coming into the country, or whether it was a deliberate policy to prevent a large, heavily Kurdish area from growing in the country is hard to say for sure, but it seems likely to me that an element of both considerations came into play.

However hard things were for the Kurdish refugees in Iran though, they were harder for those who stayed in Iraq. Let us start with that simple decision, to stay or to go, and how people made it, because that is a decision that split families and tore apart the social bonds of villages. It is a decision that saw one brother staying and one going, even within my family, and could be seen in many ways as the first step of the breakdown of the strength of my people in Iraq.

What kind of considerations made someone go? What considerations made them stay? I have already discussed above the notion of weathering the storm; the idea that many people may have felt that, however bad things were about to get, they had been through them before. There may also have been an element of pride involved. Although Kurds live across a wide spread of territory, particular tribes were often focussed on more specific areas at this point. There were more Barzani in Iraq, for example, than in Iran, Turkey or Syria. That simple connection to a sense of home may have been enough to make many people stay.

It seems likely though that by far the biggest factors would have been the time, knowledge, and capacity to leave. Knowledge, I have looked at to some extent above, yet there is a difference between a general sense of something coming and a specific understanding of a threat. Not everybody may have understood the extent of the threat coming, or at least, they may not have understood it in time to flee.

Time was crucial. Remember that we are not talking about a decision made over many months here. When I say that Saddam's forces moved north, that is perhaps slightly misleading. Many of those forces would have already been in the area, since they were actively engaged with both the Iranians and the peshmerga until the Algiers Accords came into force. While others came to join them from the south when it came to rounding up my people, many troops were already in place. Although much of the removal of the population did not take place until 1978, those who did not escape in the early days quickly found themselves surrounded by too many soldiers to do so at all. In particular, the Iraqi army instituted strict border controls. There were still ways through the mountains, of course, but it meant that for most people, the trip was much more difficult.

The final factor was the physical ability to make the trip. Yes, it would have been psychologically difficult for my people to leave behind everything they had built up in their lives, but it was also physically demanding. Men, women and children had to flee over the mountains, through often harsh conditions, without the time to adequately prepare. Even though the Kurds know the mountains as well as anyone, not everyone survived the journey. People had to assess whether they and their families could successfully make the journey, and whether they would be able to move fast enough to avoid the advancing troops.

That is a decision that my family had to make. In Sherwan, probably more than half of the families left the village, heading for the Iranian border. The decision for my family, however, was far from easy. I had just been born, with the result that neither I nor my mother were able to travel. Yet my family were Barzani, close supporters of Mullah Mustafa, and in many cases peshmerga.

My father was actually away fighting when the decision came. They knew that if there were going to be reprisals, they would be among those targeted.

That is why my family split. My father was away fighting. My uncle took his family to Iran, but he also took my older brother, who I did not see again for more than sixteen years, when the peshmerga finally freed us from the camps. It must have been such a difficult decision for my family, deciding to stay despite everything they probably suspected might happen next.

What did happen next? The answer to that is that the Iraqi army, as part of its 'counter-insurgency' campaign, destroyed more than six hundred villages. It killed some of the inhabitants, although in this initial phase, the concerns seem to have been to move people into more concentrated areas and remove villages around the border.

Some of my earliest memories are of the Eastern European made trucks they used to transport us when they came to our village. Everyone was scared, because we thought they were coming to kill us. We were able to take almost nothing with us. The lie they told was that everything would be provided for us when we reached our destination, though I doubt that anyone really believed them. The truth was simply that no one had a choice. The only alternative to going was trying to fight, and the people left in the village were not soldiers.

We know now that the soldiers from Bagdad destroyed the villages that they cleared completely in this phase. Every inhabitant in those six hundred villages was forced to leave. Those who tried to resist were killed unless they were able to run away. The houses were torn down, and anything there that might conceivably have helped someone trying to live there was taken. There are reports from the later village clearances of the Anfal that communications cables were torn up and livestock slaughtered. While this was not on the same scale, it certainly involved many of the same tactics. The idea was not just to remove the inhabitants from a village, but to ensure that they could not come back to rebuild the way they had so many times before.

One effect of this was to create a zone along Iraq's borders free from Kurdish villages. The intention, or at least the official justification, may have been to make it difficult for peshmerga to pass back and forth between Iran and Iraq to continue their fight. One difficulty in examining the actions of the regime in this genocide is always that there seems to have been more than one motivation for each step it took. This initial destruction of villages is no exception. It served as a reprisal, as a deterrent against future uprisings, as a way to concentrate the Kurds, and particularly the Barzani, in less rural areas where they could be watched, and as a way of placing the border regions in military control.

What they did next shows something of the confusion of aims there. They placed many of us in camps surrounded by military outposts, which we could not leave without risking death or disappearance. They concentrated us in those areas to watch us. Yet at the same time, they took pains to split us up, with multiple camps around numerous Kurdish cities, and even further afield. From a combination of official records and the stories of survivors, we know, for example, that large numbers of Kurds were transported all the way to the south of Iraq, to largely Arab controlled areas. Four hundred families found themselves transported all the way to Abu Graib, to what became an infamous prison.

In this first phase of forced movement to camps, the regime sometimes referred to them as refugee camps, and sometimes as collectives. The idea implied was either of removal to a safe place, or of the Kurds getting to take part in a soviet style vision of utopian vision. Both approaches are clearly lies, but their use does illustrate an important point, which is the role the official propaganda machine played throughout the process of genocide.

My family was removed to two camps in turn, both relatively close to Erbil. First, we were taken to the Seberan camp, and then to the Baherka camp. There were also other camps around Erbil, including the Harir and Qush Tappa camps. The initial phase seems to have been one of assessment, or possibly of temporary containment while a more permanent solution was sought. Certainly, the Baherka camp was not finished by the time we were brought to it. It also seems to have marked a distinction between one large camp and many smaller ones, splitting us still further after the initial destruction of our way of life.

In total, not including those who fled ahead of the destruction, this phase of rounding up my people seems to have involved the displacement, capture or killing of upwards of a quarter of a million people. It is for this reason that I want to argue for it forming a part of the later genocide, rather than a separate counter insurgency campaign, or even a precursor to it. The key here is continuity.

As I have suggested above, even writers who have agreed that the Anfal and Halabja were part of an attempt at genocide have tended to treat the events of the 1970s separately; as the aftermath of a revolt or a counter-insurgency campaign. I would like to suggest that it is an approach that doesn't allow us to fully understand the situation for a couple of reasons.

The first is that it cuts us off from any sense

of context when looking at later events. We see the attack on Halabja, and it seems like a one off until we look at the Anfal campaign before it. We see the Anfal campaign, and it seems like a few months of evil madness on the part of the regime if we do not look at what came before. Yet it is not something that came out of nowhere. Murder on that scale does not just happen. It is something that takes planning, preparation, and official will to produce. Understanding the 1970s as part of the process of producing that genocide is crucial if we want to understand the genocide itself. The Anfal might have been the culmination of the process of genocide, but the nineteen-seventies were both the starting point and the test bed. They show the point at which the intention came into being and at which the strategies employed were first tested on a smaller scale.

Crucially, we must also remember that the Anfal and Halabja themselves were not neatly one thing. They were attempts to destroy the Kurds, but they also came in a wider context of violence. If we dismiss the displacements of the 1970s as a counter-insurgency campaign, then how should we characterise the later events? They took place in the middle of a war against Iran, after all, and in the context of Kurdish fighters acting against the regime. If we suggest that the 1970s did not constitute part of a genocide, then there is a real danger that we have to go on to minimise what clearly *was* a genocide in the next decade.

So I want to argue for continuity between the events in the wake of the Algiers Accord and those of 1987-8. There are certainly good reasons for doing so. The methods were similar. As we will see, the destruction of villages formed a cornerstone of the Anfal. So did the removal of their inhabitants to camps and the splitting of Kurdish communities in an attempt to destroy their identity. If the scale of the killing was far greater in the 1980s, accompanied by the use of chemical weapons, that does not mean that the aftermath of the Algiers Accords was free from killing. In any case, we must remember that the forced displacement of a population is itself a crime against humanity just as serious as that of genocide.

Yet I know I must address the obvious question here: if the events of the 1970s are connected to those of 1987-8, why did the murder of so many people only take place during the Anfal and not before? To put it another way, if Saddam Hussein always intended the mass murder of my people, why did he and those who agreed with him not do it in 1975?

There are essentially two answers to this. Both seem to fit the facts, and so I will present both here. Both also maintain the idea of continuity with the events of the 1980s. The first of these possibilities is that Saddam, or at least his party, was not initially looking to destroy the Kurdish people in the sense of committing genocide. Instead, this approach is to suggest that the Iraqi government was looking for a solution to the 'problem' of the Kurds, seeing each rebellion to try to get a free Kurdish homeland as evidence of a failure to solve that problem and thus proof of the need for more extreme tactics.

Looked at like that, we can see almost a progression in the actions of the regime. First, Saddam went to try to broker a deal in 1970. That failed with a renewed Kurdish rebellion, so after the Algiers Accords, he moved to breaking up Kurdish villages, driving many from the country and putting many more in camps. From there, the regime moved to creating prohibited zones. That failed to solve the 'problem', so in 1983, it moved up to targeting men and boys of fighting age for mass murder. When that didn't stop all opposition to the regime, it moved up to full scale genocide during the Anfal.

The evidence in favour of this explanation is that the main escalations towards genocide have coincided with periods of Kurdish revolt or turbulence with Iran. They came after the 1973-5 revolt, after a brief uprising in 1983, and at the height of the Iran-Iraq war in 1988. There is also evidence in the targeting of much of the initial killing at men of fighting age.

This is not the explanation I believe to be the correct one, but I have included it in the interests of balance. There *is* evidence for it, and you may feel that it is the explanation that best fits the evidence. My own view on what happened takes a different approach, and rests primarily on the capacity of the regime to carry out its plans, focussing on what we know of Saddam Hussein's personality.

He was not a man who was willing to forgive slights, or anything that he saw as a betrayal. He was famously generous to the people of his own village and tribe, as well as to members of his inner circle. Yet he was just as famously focussed on destroying anyone who stood against him, even years after the fact. It seems likely that the rebellion after he brokered the 1970 peace deal was not just a political event for Saddam. It was a personal affront. A betrayal I believe he did not forgive. After all, in speaking about the 8,000 Barzani men and boys murdered in 1983, he said that they "betrayed their country and have gone to hell."

My belief is that, for Saddam and for some of those around him, if not for the regime as a whole, the intention was always to utterly destroy the Kurds. The question was simply one of what they were politically able to do and get away with at the time. It is notable, for example, that the first wave of village de-populations came after Saddam became the de-facto head of the country in 1976, while that process continued as he became the official president of the country.

The idea here is simply this: Saddam was not in complete control of Iraq, but his control over the country increased gradually over the two decades since the failure of the 1970 agreement. As his control increased, as he surrounded himself with more and more eager supporters, as he rid himself of those people who would have balked at the thought of mass murder, and as excuses came along for him to do it, he was able to take more and more pronounced steps towards his eventual goal.

The evidence for this comes partly in the correlation between the growth of Saddam's power and the growth of the violence. It also helps to explain why steps forward took place in times of war or rebellion, when the regime was less likely to be subject to close scrutiny. It does a lot to explain the 'prohibited zones' where people were not allowed to go to see what was happening, and it does something to explain the regime's emphasis on a simultaneous propaganda campaign to protect itself.

Ultimately, we may need to adopt some blend of these two models if we are to explain the full range of approaches taken across the regime.

I fully believe that Saddam intended to destroy my people, yet I can also see that not everyone within his regime would have felt the same. Many of those 'moderates' (if such a word can be applied to people complicit in mass murder), may have been carried by the need to solve a 'problem' of repeated rebellion.

Whichever approach you decide fits the evidence better, I hope it is clear by now that some sort of continuity of intent fits the evidence we have. The regime always intended to either kill the Kurds or solve the 'problem' of them. In the 1970s, it was not just fighting a counter-insurgency campaign. It was taking the first steps on a road that would lead to the use of chemical weapons against its citizens.

One of those steps was that I grew up in what was, effectively, a prison camp.

3

The Camp

Today, when I go to Kurdistan, the camp they took us to has been swallowed up by the redevelopment of the country. Where other places might want to create a monument to a painful past, Kurdistan is busy creating its future, with the result that most of the four hundred or so units of the Baherka camp have been replaced by modern houses or office blocks.

Because they came to take us from our village when I was very young, all the memories I have of growing up are of the camp. From the time I was old enough to really remember anything until I was very nearly an adult I was trapped in the Baherka camp outside Erbil, hemmed in by razor wire, machine gun posts and watch towers. There were army camps not far from us in several directions, effectively surrounding us with Saddam's troops for upwards of a decade.

That was how I grew up. In this chapter I'm going to set out some of what life was like in the camps from day to day, how they were arranged and how they ran. I'm going to look a little more at prohibited zones and what they meant for those Kurds outside the camps. I'm also going to go into the events of 1983, which fit in with the general on-going oppression of the camps.

Let's start with the basic physical layout of the camp. It lay to the south of Erbil, close enough to be monitored by the military bases there, yet still far enough outside the main city that it was surrounded by farms and fields.

It was a rough square picked out because no one else wanted it and surrounded by chain link fences, topped with razor wire to prevent anyone escaping, with watch towers and military patrols further out to kill anyone who tried. Until I was sixteen, that fence marked the outer limit of the world as I knew it.

Eventually, there were housing 'units' arranged in neat rows within the surrounding square of the fence.

When we first got there, despite having been kept in a holding camp previously, they were not finished, with the result that we had to spend winter using tents as shelter, trying to finish the structures ourselves with whatever materials we could get.

The units started off identical, but quickly became more individual as people finished them in different ways, using whatever they could. Typically, they had corrugated iron roofs and mud-brick walls.

There were generally four families living in each unit. With relatively large families and lots of children, there was often very little space within the housing units, and certainly no sense of privacy. Each house came with a small garden, which was in reality just a patch of dirt out of which we tried to eke as many vegetables and other foodstuffs as possible to stop ourselves from starving. Frequently, it didn't work.

For the adults there, the camp seems to have been defined by two primary emotions: fear and boredom. Each day was the same as the last, with no chance of achieving anything permanent or even just *better,* yet at the same time, there was always that sense of waiting for something to happen. Knowing that the people who had put us into camps might decide any day to simply kill us, and the first warning we would have would be when they showed up and started doing it.

Put like that, it must have taken tremendous courage for the adults there to have kept going with their lives.

For them to have tried to keep things as normal as possible for their families, and to ensure that their children grew up as well as was possible in such an impossible environment. It must have taken a lot of strength not to give in to despair in a situation that seems to have been deliberately designed to instil it.

For the children there, the camp was simply all we knew. As far as we were concerned, it was normal to grow up living that way. As far as we knew, every child in the world lived behind a chain link fence and had nothing. The way children always seem to in harsh environments, we still found ways to be children, even if only briefly. We would, for example, make footballs out of old socks and kick those around, or play games around the housing units with other children from our families or nearby. There was even a school of sorts, run by an Arabic teacher brought in specifically to do so.

Yet there was so much that we didn't have. The most basic things were missing in the camps, with the result that even as children, we had to work hard just to help our families survive. I remember having to climb up onto the roof of our unit to clear off water every time it rained, because the makeshift, flat roof wouldn't have stood up to water for long if we'd left it.

I mentioned the kind of football we used above. We certainly never had any real toys, not just because our parents were never in a position to afford them, but because they could never go anywhere to get them.

We rarely if ever had new clothes, with the result that those we wore for school were patched and mended, despite being supposedly our best clothes.

Today, I see children in Kurdistan and elsewhere who have so much more. They have nice school uniforms, good educations, opportunities that most of us would never have dreamed of when we were stuck in the camps. Even simple things like being educated in our native language weren't available to us. Yet often these days, you hear children complaining that they don't have the latest electronic gadget or because their parents won't allow them to do exactly as they please.

I try not to get too annoyed by that, though. In many ways, it is a good thing. If we live in a world where the worst our children will have to worry about is whether they have everything that their friends have, then that means we have come so far from the days when I and my friends were brought up inside the camps. I'm actually quite jealous in many ways. If I had been born just ten or fifteen years later, it would have been at a golden time for Kurdistan, and I might have had everything growing up that these children have.

Yet there seems to be one thing that I and the other children who were brought up in the camps have: a sense of determination. So many of those who were brought up there have gone on to be successful professionals, including doctors and lawyers. It is like they are determined to show the world that despite everything, they are still there. It is an attitude that in some ways applies to the whole of Kurdistan.

Yet I'd like to say again that for us at the time, the camps seemed normal. They were simply how things were. Just as importantly, we didn't have a great deal of contact with the outside world. The idea with the camps was not just to keep us in a concentrated area, it was to isolate us and cut us off from the world.

Some of that was achieved very simply, because it was hard for people to travel back and forth in and out of the camps. It wasn't impossible, because there are instances where peshmerga made their way inside to deliver messages, but it was always risky for them to do so, and in general we were cut off from news of people elsewhere. Kurds living in Erbil sometimes managed to sneak up to the fence to supply people in the camp with additional food or things they needed, but again, that was far from constant and the risks were great. The areas immediately around camps were usually designated as prohibited zones, meaning that people found in them could be shot on sight.

There was some information trickling in from the outside through one anomaly in the camp: a small number of the people there had access to TV and radio. There was even a Kurdish language TV station in the region, set up by Bagdad as part of the failed process of regional autonomy. In theory, that should have allowed us to learn more about the world beyond the fences of the camp, but in practice, it served primarily as a vehicle for propaganda about Saddam and the ruling party. We were told even as children that we couldn't trust what we heard there.

That propaganda aspect was a big part of the camps, forming two corners of a triangle with the destruction of the Kurds at its apex. The camps contained us and made us easy targets for further oppression. We will come to the attempts to destroy us physically soon, but propaganda and related aspects were aimed at destroying us culturally, removing the idea of Kurdishness and instilling the idea of loyalty to Saddam. It was a propaganda campaign aimed, not just at those of us in the camps, but at all those in Kurdistan.

There are, for example, plenty of examples of Saddam making official visits to villages in Kurdistan. He would dress up in traditional Kurdish costumes, hand out gifts, and essentially try to appear as someone who understood my people even while his regime was taking actions designed to destroy them. He tried to cultivate an image of benevolence even among people he considered traitors to be killed.

That propaganda extended to the camps. There was a small school in our camp, run by an Arab teacher. Every Thursday as children, we had to sing songs praising Saddam and his achievements. We had to wear special Saddam badges to show our 'support' for the dictator, and we had to pay for them each week. As children, we had no choice in the matter, and it was coupled with the already Saddam-friendly contents of whatever radio or TV coverage we could get access to, in a concerted propaganda effort.

An effort to do what, though? Can we seriously say that Saddam's advisors and ministers expected that with enough effort, they would be able to make Kurdish children into citizens loyal to him? That singing a few songs would override the effects of being kept in a town sized cage by Iraq's rulers? It is in many ways one of the more chilling elements of the regime that perhaps they *did* expect that. Even in Hitler's Germany, where the propaganda machine has generally been regarded as one of the more complete of modern times, the aim was never to make the Jews like the man who murdered them, yet that is roughly the equivalent of what the Iraqi government was trying to do in the 1980s.

Perhaps the existence of a propaganda machine like this one lends some credence to the idea that Saddam was trying to solve the 'problem' of the Kurds in any way he could. It suggests that by coupling a broader policy of oppression with a 're-education' programme, he may have been attempting to eliminate a generation of my people willing to rebel against him while simultaneously brainwashing the following generation to be what he saw as good citizens. Which is to say, citizens fanatically loyal to the idea of both him and his Iraq. Neither idea truly took root, however, which means that it seems equally valid to look at things another way, and see the propaganda simply as a way of keeping the camps quiet and free from rebellion long enough for the government to move to the next stage of its programme of genocide.

To some extent, the element of propaganda in the camps shows us one important point, which is that the events of the camps were not the only element occurring at the time to contribute to the isolation and destruction of my people. Just as some of the propaganda affecting the camps also affected the wider country, so to there were other policies that had a dramatic effect on Kurdistan in the period.

One was the presence of so called prohibited zones. The one created next to the border in the late seventies is the most obvious, but there were numerous others. Some were used around the camps, while others were used where villages had been destroyed, to prevent the inhabitants from coming back.

The essence of the protected zones was simple in theory. Anyone found within one by the military could be executed on sight. Yet their application was probably different in this period from their later use during the Anfal campaign. In that campaign, they became a tool to designate the operational areas of mass murder. Prior to that, and there can be no doubt that militarily policed prohibited areas existed prior to that, they were primarily there to denote areas of heightened security, to stop the curious from wandering too close to the borders or to the camps. I would also like to note one point of their operation here. In theory, they allowed for the execution of anyone caught within. However, the evidence seems clear that in practice during this period, the Iraqi military focussed primarily on those of my people found within them, and on men. Even during their later application during the Anfal campaign, as we shall see, there was a distinct concentration on men as the main targets.

A second policy against my people outside the camps was that of Arabization. Although, as with the prohibited zones, it not given its fullest expression until the Anfal, it was an on-going process from the late 1970s onwards. It began with a response to the disputes over Kirkuk, trying to introduce more Arabs into that city to justify the Bagdad government's claim to it, but it quickly expanded to take in the rest of Kurdistan.

It consisted of three interlinked elements: the bringing in of Arabs to the area, the promotion of trusted Arab figures to positions of importance, and pressures on the Kurds to change their culture to something more Arabic in tone.

The first two points are probably inextricable. Arabs were brought into the area from all around Iraq, but how was the regime able to persuade them to move their whole lives across the country without the violence and intimidation it employed against my people? The short answer was that it had to promise them a better life in Kurdistan, whether that came in the form of a farm to run, a job, a nice house, or something else. Arabs came to Kurdistan because it genuinely seemed to offer them an improved standard of living or a set of opportunities that they could not receive by staying where they were. Of course, this being Saddam's regime, there probably were plenty of implicit threats to go with it. When the government 'suggested' that someone might want to move north, it probably didn't need to explicitly state some of the alternatives. Yet there is a clear difference between that and the way my people were forcibly removed from their homes.

Where did these people end up? Well, in a few cases, they ended up living right next to our camp. It was surrounded by farms, none of which had Kurds working on them (they would have been executed). Instead, the farms were mostly Arab owned and run, with Arab workers. The government might have removed Kurdish families from the land, but it still needed food for its Arab population and its army. It wasn't acceptable to it to leave those farms empty.

A less overt form of Arabization came in the cultural sphere. We have already seen that elements such as Kurdish language television were in place, while Saddam's occasional propaganda trick of visiting villages in Kurdistan and playing the part of one of us meant that there was, curiously, never the same sense of the country ignoring us the way Turkey did. Yet there *were* attempts to drastically change our culture. Education throughout Kurdistan, particularly any form of higher education, was delivered in Arabic. The arts and intellectual life were conducted on an official level in Arabic. Even supposedly 'Kurdish' elements focussed on history rather than any continuing tradition, suggesting that it was not relevant to the modern world. I have already written about the Arabic teacher who came to the camp to teach us. An Arabic teacher, conducting lessons in Arabic, for a camp full of Kurdish children.

The intention seems to have been a long term one. Clearly, the regime had decided that

nothing could be done with the current generation of Kurds, yet it seems that the idea was in
place to ensure that in a couple of generations,
any Kurds left thought of themselves as Arabs.
It was a less obvious approach to eliminating
our culture than the one taken in Turkey, yet it
was probably more likely to have been successful had it been allowed to continue long term,
because it wasn't as easy to identify and resist
simply by saying "I am Kurdish."

It is worth pointing out here that Arabic
influences weren't the only outside ones being
brought in. Where additional skills were
needed, or where it would make more money,
Saddam and his cronies seem to have had no
problem bringing in foreign assistance. The
regime seems to have been unable or unwilling
to find sufficient Arab farmers to fill the farms
around our camp, for example, with the result
that at least one of them was staffed by people I
now know to have been Australian. As children,
we stared at them through the fence and called
them English, on the basis that it was what we
called all Westerners.

The presence of these Australians makes it
clear to me that, despite the limitations on access
around the camps, and despite the threats to life
of the prohibited zones, at least some foreigners
got to see what was happening in my country at
that time. Indeed, there were a small number of

news reports and documentary pieces covering the issue, such as Gwynne Roberts' *Forbidden Frontiers* for ITN news[9]. I can say with confidence, therefore, that the world was aware of what was going on throughout.

That seems even to be true of one of the most painful episodes in the camps, the 1983 massacre of approximately 8,000 men and boys from the Barzani tribe, mostly taken from the camps. It came in the context of a renewed Kurdish rebellion, but how can that serve as any sort of excuse for the regime? It cannot, and the events of 1983 in many ways mark the transition from a government policy of containment in the camps to one of mass murder. They pre-date the Anfal by five years, yet they still form part of the process of genocide.

I was still no more than nine, but I remember the day they came for us clearly. My mother thought that when they came with trucks they had just come to harass us, the way the occasionally did. Perhaps they had come to take men away to force them into the army, or perhaps they had come to take away one or two as dissidents to beat them or worse. It says a lot about the circumstances in the camp that we thought of that kind of thing as normal.

Yet I remember feeling like this was something

9	http://www.rwfworld.com/productions/middle-east/forbidden-frontiers/

different. Perhaps that is just being wise after the event, remembering what happened next, but I do recall *telling* my mother that I didn't think this was normal, because there were too many soldiers. I think perhaps children have that sense for when things are not right, or perhaps adults are simply far more aware than children of the things they cannot change, and so try to persuade themselves that they are all right simply so that they do not have to face up to them.

I remember the soldiers rounding up the men. They searched the whole compound, and I saw men jabbing bayonets into sacks of flour to make sure that no one was hiding inside. They didn't even give a warning to get out, so if anyone had been hiding there, they would have died. They told the rest of the men that they had to go for a meeting with Saddam, and I think that many of the men assumed that they were being taken away to be Jhash, or Kurdish fighters in the Iraqi army.

Similar events must have been taking place in other parts of the country. Some may have evaded capture then, but not many. My father tells the story of avoiding being taken by hopping down off the truck that came for him, claiming that he was just going to get his sons. The soldiers believed him, probably laughing at this gullible man who had believed their lie about men needing to see Saddam so utterly that he was going to bring his sons to die with him. I wonder if they were still laughing a couple of hours later while he was making his escape?

They say now that the mass murder of Barzani people in 1983 was intended to target men of fighting age, perhaps to prevent them from rising up against the regime, the way peshmerga outside the camps had around that time. How the regime thought Barzani men could have risen from inside a camp is unclear, but that seems to have been the justification they used for their violence. What is important to remember, however, is that the determination of 'fighting age' was done largely by eye rather than by any formal assessment of age.

I remember that there was an Iraqi army officer in an elaborate uniform complete with plenty of medals. He had a long stick that would have normally been used for beating anyone who got in his way. On that day though, it became an improvised measuring stick. It is one of the few times I was grateful to be small for my age. I had friends the same age as me who were nevertheless considered to be big and strong enough to take, yet when he dragged me out of the line and measured me against this stick, he shoved me back with the words "Bastard's no good." Those were the words that saved my life.

We're now fairly sure about what happened

to the 8,000 who were taken, including several of my cousins. Saddam said that they "betrayed their country and went to hell." In other words, they were murdered. Most probably, according to evidence from witnesses, they were taken to the desert in the south of the country. There, they would have been lined up on the edge of mass graves and machine gunned, with bulldozers filling in the graves without checking if anyone had survived the initial round of violence. That is what I survived only by being a little too young; a little too short.

After 1983, the camps became a stranger place than ever. It was almost impossible to find a woman there who wasn't in mourning clothes for her husband or one of her sons. It changed the social dynamics of the camps dramatically. Women had to run the families in the camps, in contrast to much of the rest of the region, simply because there were no men old enough to do so in the traditional fashion.

In the wake of 1983, we started to move around the camp, never staying in one place long. My father and my brothers were still alive, and the authorities wanted them. They threatened to kill us if they did not give themselves up. That is not an isolated phenomenon. Indeed, I believe that one reason they did not kill everyone in the camp was because it left them with hostages to use against any relatives left outside.

They would come and search our home every few days, along with the homes of other residents they believed might be hiding potential peshmerga. It was something that intensified significantly over the years, so that by the end of the 1980s we were almost constantly on the move, staying with this family and then that family to confuse the guards. We weren't alone in that. Quite a few families moved around from house to house, either because they believed that if they didn't they would be taken, or because they wanted to keep it unclear as to exactly which family members were there.

If that sounds hard to do, remember that this was not a well ordered prison camp where the guards were watching every moment of our lives or where every detail about us was well known. It was more like a village with no amenities or facilities, surrounded by barbed wire fences and guard towers. The guards were there to keep us from getting out or to take specific people, but they were not there to run our lives for us. It would have been too much work for them to do it. All they had to do was sit back and wait for the next time Saddam wanted to murder the inhabitants, and I do believe it would have come again. Perhaps, like taking a census, there would have been a bout of genocide every ten years to deal with any Kurds old enough to fight back. Thankfully, we will never know for sure.

It was in the mid-late eighties that my mother started pretending that two of my brothers were dead, wearing mourning clothes for them and telling any guards who demanded to know where they were that they had died in the Anfal. It was the best way to keep them safe at the time, but it was also a mark of the way the events outside the camp affected life there. We heard something of the outside world, and it changed the details of our fear about what might happen, but it only altered things from day to day a little.

That may seem strange, since I have previously spent time arguing that the camps were part of the wider campaign of genocide and I intend to spend more time doing it later. It might seem impossible that life should change so little during a period when my people were being murdered on a massive scale. If we were locked away in a camp and that camp was intended to be part of the destruction of the Kurds, shouldn't we have been among the first to die? Yet I would argue that it is precisely *because* we were locked away that the regime didn't do so. It was too busy killing those of my people who were still living normal lives in their villages, or moving them into camps like ours. Perhaps it was simply that they had already done to us most of the things they planned on doing to others of my people.

In one way, when looked at like that, perhaps I was even lucky to be in the camp when I was. That seems insane, I know, yet what were the alternatives? Growing up in a Kurdish village that might have been wiped out completely by soldiers or by poison gas? Being dumped in one of the later camps where there was literally nothing but desert and no attempt made to provide the most rudimentary housing, the way those put in camps during the Anfal were? Perhaps I would have been 'disappeared' for belonging to the Barzani, or just for walking in the wrong place. The camp is easily the worst place I have ever been, yet perhaps there is also a case for saying that being there kept me away from so many things that might have been even worse.

Let us leave that thought, though, and return to the question of genocide. Were the camps a part of an overall programme of genocide? Was the camp I was kept in? More generally, what were the camps for? What role did they play, and why did the Iraqi regime go to such trouble to keep us in them?

I fervently believe that the camps *did* form a part of the process of genocide. They were certainly a crime against humanity in their own right, representing part of the forced displacement of my people, along with their mistreatment.

Yet more than that, they also facilitated genocide.

If you subscribe to the idea I have set out that perhaps the regime was trying to solve the 'problem' of the Kurds in increasingly violent ways, then the camps represent a step along that path. A step that involved the first use of organised mass murder by the regime in a controlled environment. It was the moment it switched over from murder as a by-product of rounding people up to a cold blooded, calculating act that cost the lives of more than 8,000 people. The camps in that model represent another step along the road to the Anfal.

If you see genocide as the eventual intention of the government, as I do, then the camps represent both a mechanism for performing mass murder more easily on an on-going basis, and to some extent a trial of the methods that would later be employed, with that mixture of murder, displacement, imprisonment and propaganda. Although not all of those elements were aimed at killing Kurds, they were all aimed at destroying the Kurds as a people. The camps provided an environment where that destruction could continue through the destruction of our culture, through the separation of my people from their traditional lands, through the Arabization of succeeding generations, and through the periodic mass murder of the population without having to worry about villages fleeing or fighting back.

Life in the camps was hard. It changed families, and it may have done much to change the way many of my people look at the world. It certainly had a number of important effects on me. In 1983, it also gave us a taste of just what the Bagdad government was capable of, with the murder of so many of the Barzani. Yet even compared to that, what would come next was worse.

4

The Anfal

'Anfal' has gone from a noun among my people to a verb. To Anfal has become synonymous with mass murder and genocide. It lives on in our memories as the single worst period of atrocities we have suffered in our histories, yet it is a genocide that is considerably less well known than many others. Even people who have heard about Saddam killing the Kurds may not always know the term, because often their focus is on Halabja rather than the wider campaign around it.

Anfal translates into English as "the spoils of war", and is taken from a passage in the Qur'an where newly converted tribal warriors argue about dividing up what they have taken in the aftermath of battle. That much is raised by almost every writer who has commented on the Anfal campaign. I'd like to take a moment to look deeper at that choice of name and how it relates to the campaign.

There are a couple of different ways of looking at this name, chosen by Bagdad. We could see it as the Iraqi forces taking the spoils of war in the latter stages of the Iran-Iraq war of 1980-1989.

If we view it this way, then the name declares that it was almost the right of the Iraqi military to move in and destroy the civilian populations of Kurdish villages on the basis that a small number of peshmerga may have aided the Iranian forces during the war by rising up against Bagdad. Essentially, it focusses on the idea that the government's forces were moving in after the main war and taking whatever they could from the Kurds.

As an approach, it seems a little flawed, because it implies an emphasis to the campaign that was focussed on plunder, rather than destruction. There was an element of such plundering to the campaign, because the government forces took whatever they could, whether it was personal property, resources, or even Kurdish women, yet as we will see below, the emphasis seems to have been less on taking what they could than on leaving nothing behind.

Possibly, this use of the term was propaganda led. Possibly, the idea was to disguise a larger evil with a smaller one, by portraying what was intended as genocide as simply the Iraqi military taking the spoils of war in the late stages of their conflict with Iran. The government was always expert in doing exactly as much as it could get away with, and perhaps this choice of name was a reflection of that. Perhaps it realised that an *openly* genocidal campaign might be enough to invite international or other sanctions, whereas the same international community might write off the 'spoils of war' as something less, and therefore something it could forget about. It is worth remembering that Turkey was also facing a Kurdish revolt at the time, and was taking repressive measures to put it down. So, for as long as Iraq's approach appeared roughly proportionate to Turkey's, it was unlikely that the international community was ever going to get involved. Avoiding the appearance of a full campaign of genocide may have been enough to achieve that.

That is one sense of the name. There is another, more chilling way of looking at it, however. In the section of the Qur'an the term is taken from, it is warrior tribes who are arguing over the spoils. That choice of name, therefore, may have been the government's way of saying that the largely tribal Kurds were about to receive the 'spoils' of their involvement in the Iran-Iraq war, in the form of extermination. It is certainly an approach to the name more consistent with what I saw of the Bagdad government at the time, and with what happened next.

Of course, all of these elements may have had a role to play, depending on the circumstances in which it was being used. In many ways *that* is the key point about the Anfal: that it was a multi-faceted campaign that presented different faces to different people. To the international community, it seems to have been something to be largely dismissed as none of their business. To many members of the Iraqi army, it was an opportunity to engage in plunder, rape and other crimes with impunity. For my people, it was a campaign of destruction that killed us on a scale not previously seen in Iraq, and matched only by some of the most serious genocides elsewhere.

So, what was the Anfal? That is the first point where reality is a little more complex than the popular image. It is generally referred to as one thing; one sweeping wave of destruction that caught up hundreds of thousands of my people. Certainly, there was continuity, and it is perfectly valid to refer to the whole thing as one coherent programme of genocide. At the same time, however, it must be understood that we are not talking about a single campaign in the military sense.

In that sense, there were a number of distinct phases to what we now refer to simply as the Anfal, all taking place in 1987-9. The first was a kind of preparatory phase, not technically part of the Anfal as such, but involving many tactics aimed at the overall aim of destroying the Kurds. These included the destruction of villages and the establishment of numerous additional prohibited zones. This first phase is important and should not be ignored, both because it was in itself a sustained attack on the civilian population of Kurdistan, and because it connects the Anfal to earlier actions of the government through the use of similar tactics. It is this preparatory phase that shows us that things like the mass murder of Barzani men in 1983 were not separate incidents, but were part of an on-going campaign with consistent tactics and aims.

Schuurman emphasises that the main period of the Anfal campaign consisted of eight stages, which we will explore here[10]. The first took place in February and March 1988, the second targeted the Qara Dagh district from March to April, the third targeted the south of the country in the second half of April, the fourth took place over five days in May, targeting land to the south east of Erbil.

The fifth, sixth and seventh all took place north east of Erbil, and involved repeated assaults against the same areas between May and August. The eighth took place over two weeks from August to September, targeting the Turkish border.

We will discuss each of these phases in turn, starting with the preparatory phase and moving through them chronologically. However, first, I want to discuss a trio of points that come out

---

10   Schuurman, pp24-36

of that timing, to explore the Anfal and how it happened.

The first is that, if we focus purely on the eight phases above, rather than including the preparatory phases as I believe we should, then the Anfal moved very quickly. It took place, not just in less than a year, but in less than eight months. That speed says something about the determination of the government to wipe out the Kurds. It possibly also says something about the wider circumstances of the Iran-Iraq war, and how limited the Iraqi government's window of opportunity was. The war in that period was perhaps less intense than it had been, only a year away from its official end, so the Iraqi government had only a small space where the conflict was sufficiently low intensity to allow them to act against their own people without harming themselves militarily, while still being there to act as a cover for their actions.

Another thing the timing tells us is how carefully planned the Anfal campaign was. To have produced such a sweeping wave of violence, sometimes with just days between one section of the campaign and another, took coordination and high level planning. In other words, this was not just a series of excesses brought on by the circumstances of war. Nor was it separate from broader circumstances. Instead, it was a carefully pre-planned expression of long standing wishes on the part of Saddam Hussein and his party. The smoothness with which the Anfal was executed shows that it was not an aberration or a snap decision, but rather simply the fullest expression of attitudes and policies already in place.

Finally, there is the breadth of the campaign, taking place across wide swathes of Iraq. This suggests that it was not a reactive campaign, coming in response to any specific Kurdish rebellion. It also suggests something about the aims of the campaign. It was not to pacify territory or stop potential rebellion. Both of those would have involved campaigns in very limited spaces, possibly just along the border. The earliest actions from 1975 show that kind of approach. Those during the Anfal were much more general.

Yet I will say again that they were all part of the same thing. The Anfal was not something separate or special. It was an attempt at genocide, but calling it that must not label all the previous actions of the government as something else.

We must not say that the actions of the Anfal turn things such as 1983 or the forced displacement of my people into something that was *not* a part of an attempt to destroy my people.

We must instead see the Anfal as simply the pinnacle of an on-going campaign, and as being consistent with the same intentions that were present in 1978, 1983 and elsewhere.

With that in mind, I want to focus on the period between 1983 and 1988 first, with particular emphasis on the period from 1987 after Ali Hassan Al-Majid (Saddam Hussein's cousin, commonly called Chemical Ali) was given special powers to deal with the Kurds. As I have said in the previous chapter, for us in the camps, the period after 1983 remained surprisingly normal, inasmuch as anything in the camps was normal. We had to move around more to keep safe, and there were frequent inspections by the guards, trying to find men or just trying to harass us, but for the majority of the time, things continued largely as they had.

The same cannot be said of the outside world. Iraq was engaged in an on-going conflict with Iran, and had been since 1980. That conflict would continue throughout the events here, and in many ways helped to fuel the violence against the Kurds by persuading even more moderate voices in Saddam's government that they could not have a people with a history of rebellion around during a war if they wanted to win it.

The progress of the early 1980s also meant increasing repression in general terms, from laws against insulting the government, to the restriction of free reporting within Iraq and the gradual extension of prohibited zones to cover wider areas around the borders and the camps. It was also in this phase that much of the process of Arabization of Kurdistan began to take place, with the large scale introduction of ordinary Arabs to Kurdistan to change the balance of the population. This was particularly true around Kirkuk, where the almost totally Arab government wanted to secure the presence of loyal Arabs in a region with some of the country's most important oil resources.

What I want to emphasise here is that there was a climate of on-going repression, particularly towards my people. It might be possible to argue that we had not reached the stage of the Anfal's mass executions, village clearances and chemical weapon attacks, but we have to remember that, except for the use of chemical weapons, all of those things *had* already happened on some scale. The mass internments of 1978 used village clearances. 1983 showed the regime's willingness to use mass murder, but it was more than that. It was the ability of the regime to make people 'disappear' from day to day even after 1983. It was the constant pressure of Arab education and culture. It was the propaganda of Saddam visiting Kurdish villages, essentially laying claim to them and demanding their loyalty. It was the on-going threat to ordinary Kurdish people of being snatched or executed for any reason or none.

We rightly focus on the major events where the most people died, but the absence of such events does not mean that tyranny and murder were also absent between 1983 and 1987. Nor does it mean that the intention to destroy my people was absent. It simply means that the regime, caught up in its war with Iran and focussing on consolidating its power, was not in a position to act on the scale it wished. It had to focus on attacking my people on a smaller scale. And it worked. For every instance where thousands of people were killed, there were a thousand small ones where people were beaten or tortured, imprisoned or simply made to disappear. If the Anfal was a torrent of genocide, the period from 1983 on was it slowed to a drip.

In 1987, it came back up to a full roar. Why was that? Part of it may have been the failure of the regime to lure the key Kurdish parties, the PUK and PDK, away from their alliances with Tehran. Peshmerga continued to fight against Iraq, frequently working in coordination with Iranian regiments. I am not saying, on any level, that the actions of the regime were justified. What happened next was not aimed at combatants, and was entirely disproportionate to the on-going conflict. I am simply trying to explain why this should have happened in 1987 and not before.

So, the failure of the regime to agree terms with

Kurdish forces may have been the final element that pushed it over the edge and into the realms of a full campaign of genocide. How does that fit with the idea that the regime always intended to wipe out my people? The answer is simple. This may have been the moment when Saddam decided that he could not put the Kurds on the back burner, to be dealt with later, and decided that wiping them out was a priority.

This may also have happened in 1987 thanks to events elsewhere. I have argued before that seeing all Kurdish rebellions as part of the same thing encourages people to view the Kurds as one 'problem' to be solved. Well, in 1987, Kurds in Turkey were engaged in a campaign against the government. The *Turkish* government might not even have recognised the existence of my people, but the Iraqi one may have seen it as a sign that further Kurdish uprisings were inevitable. As I have suggested, the Turkish uprising may also have provided the opportunity for the regime to act, by distracting attention from Iraq.

Whatever the reason, 1987 was the year when things got much worse for the majority of my people. The adoption of new powers by Al-Majid began with the extension of several tactics already employed in the form of the use of prohibited zones and the placement of civilians within camps. They were exactly the tactics used in the late seventies, but on a much larger scale.

The use of prohibited areas, for example, changed substantially. Previously, they had been an idea used to force people away from the border, theoretically preventing free travel between Iraq and Iran. They had been employed that way to effectively limit the traditional peshmerga tactic of striking and then melting over the border into Iraq's neighbour, even if they had never been entirely successful. They had also been used to limit access to sensitive areas by allowing for the summary execution of anyone found in spaces around some of the camps, for example.

During the Anfal, including some of its preparatory phase, they came to be used much more aggressively. They were used around villages, and in some cases through whole regions, effectively authorising a kill on sight policy for the Iraqi military in those areas. When the destruction of villages began, they were used in the aftermath to effectively declare the former sites of Kurdish villages off limits, preventing the villagers from ever coming back and re-constructing their homes.

The forced movement of my people also increased in scale compared to the initial efforts in the 1970s. At the start of the period 1987-1988, there were more than 4,600 villages in Kurdistan. By the end of the Anfal, around 4,000 of those had been destroyed. Many of the inhabitants were killed, and many more sent to what were supposedly camps like ours. In fact, they were simply patches of desert without even the basic structures that greeted us on our arrival in 1978. Many people starved to death or died from disease in conditions that were no longer simply about rounding up my people, but which were about destroying them.

When we talk about the destruction of villages and the shoot on sight orders of the prohibited zones, we should remember how complete they were. Every structure in targeted villages was removed, including schools and mosques. Telephone lines were torn up and livestock slaughtered. Livestock in prohibited zones were also shot whenever spotted, to attempt to starve any Kurds remaining in those areas.

In all, the period from 1987 consisted of an on-going campaign of repression against my people that included tens of thousands of deaths, detentions and disappearances, even before the regime's full plan for the Anfal campaign was in place. That is why I feel that this first phase must be considered a full part of the campaign as a whole, even if it was not seen as such by its designers.

Let's consider the detail of the campaign now. The preparatory phase took almost a year. From the smoothness with which the Anfal campaign was executed, and from the documents left behind by the regime following its overthrow, we can see that much of that time must have been spent trying out what came next. Initial preparations were made, and elements such as the prohibited zones were put in place to lend an air of legality to what was going to happen. The regime probably wanted to be able to say that it had given civilians fair warning, that it was only targeting insurgents, and that its actions were legally justified, if only by the legal instruments put in place by Saddam authorising the prohibited zones. That people would not be able to leave their homes or entire regions of the country was not mentioned, but the regime must have been aware of it. Indeed, that was its intention.

What follows next is a discussion of Schuurman's eight stages of the Anfal, and the tactics used. It is one of the most complete summaries of what happened, and so is worth drawing on here.[11] From the first phase of the official Anfal campaign, the regime resorted to the use of chemical weapons against civilians and peshmerga alike, bombing the Jafati Valley region with a mixture of chemical compounds that produced a range of symptoms in those exposed to them, most commonly including

---

11   *Ibid.*

blackened skin, irritated eyes, and difficulty breathing. This was probably something of a trial run for the regime, since there seem to have been relatively few fatalities as a result of the attacks in this phase, and only a few hundred wounded.

The Anfal against the Qara Dagh block involved significantly larger numbers, and combined chemical attacks with the established tactics of village clearances and arbitrary arrests or executions. It was also targeted at one of the primary food producing regions of Kurdistan, effectively making it harder for the civilian population of the wider region to support itself even as the campaign wiped out that of the specific region it was targeting.

The tactics in this case were simple. The regime had established in the first stage of the Anfal that chemical attacks alone would not have the level of impact that they required. The low casualty count for Jafati was partly down to a less densely populated environment, but mostly because people knew enough from their experience with the Iraqi military to run from the attack and to cover their faces while doing so. To counter this, Saddam's troops used the chemical attacks, not as the primary way of inflicting casualties, but as a way to force people to move from their homes into spaces where they could be more easily killed or captured.

In general, as in 1983, men of so called fighting age were the first killed, but there are also many accounts of women and children disappearing.

In the Third Anfal, targeting the Germian plain South East of Kirkuk, there seems to have been a particular focus on killing everyone regardless of age or gender. Although there were certainly many captives taken, the troops seem to have been far more indiscriminate than they were elsewhere, using a combination of chemical weapons and the simple storming of villages to kill as much of the population as possible in the first phase of the attacks, generally capturing only those who managed to survive and run. It is a mark of how carefully planned the Anfal was by this point that the government forces designed things to run in that way, blocking off escape routes so that those running from the slaughter would end up being captured.

There are also reports of the use of propaganda to try to trick people into surrendering at this point. Men, in particular, were encouraged to give in by being told that their 'punishment' would simply be to have to serve in the Iraqi military. If that seems far-fetched, remember that Kurdish men have been drafted in to serve in the military for decades, and that even the Anfal campaign involved the use of the *Jahsh*, those Kurds fighting for the regime. Indeed, their use may well have been a deliberate ploy to convince others that surrendering would be a good thing, since after all, they would be surrendering to fellow Kurds.

The fourth stage, focussing on land southeast of Erbil, consisted of similar basic tactics, though with perhaps a higher reliance on dropping chemical weapons by air. Indeed, although this was a phase during which there were lower casualties from those chemical weapons, that comes in the context of a slightly smaller number of targeted villages overall, and it does seem from the outside like this was a point where the tactics of the regime returned to the initial focus of using chemical weapons to kill, rather than just to drive people towards the army.

Stages five, six and seven highlight either the effectiveness of the regime's brutality as a whole, or the ineffectiveness of its tactics, depending on which way they are looked at. All targeted the same area, north-east of Erbil. That they had to take multiple passes over the same area may perhaps suggest that the tactics employed, with their increasing focus on pure chemical weapons use, were perhaps not as effective as the more total destruction in earlier phases. Alternatively, it may simply be that with the existing destruction of the countryside, there may not have been many Kurds left in the area to target. Saddam's direct orders for the sixth and seventh Anfals to take place perhaps suggest his dissatisfaction with the progress of the fifth.

The eighth Anfal took place after the temporary cessation of hostilities between Iran and Iraq on the 8th of August. This final Anfal consisted of one of the heaviest chemical weapons attacks to date, targeting forty-nine villages in the Badinan region. It seems to have been the most direct attempt to use chemical weapons as the primary instrument of killing in all of the Anfals, although again, secondary issues such as capture while fleeing or dying in the process of escaping appear to have caused many more deaths.

What threads link these disparate attacks? One that comes up again and again is the use of chemical weapons. Indeed, for many writers, the split between those attacks using chemical weapons and those taking place using solely conventional means seems to be the main justification for seeing the Anfal as a break with the past, rather than a continuation of it. We will see in the next chapter that the use of chemical weapons was very important, and probably one of the main factors influencing the eventual involvement of foreign powers in the country, but can we really claim that a change in the weapons used equals a change in the intentions of those using them?

This is particularly the case when it appears

that many of the most effective elements of the attacks were actually the conventional ones; the ones that the regime had tried before against the Barzani, and on a smaller scale. Throughout the Anfal, the phases that appear to have had the highest death toll are the ones where the emphasis was on driving the population towards well controlled points of capture or execution by conventional forces.

Another thread that we can draw out of the Anfal is the emphasis on the destruction of villages. Again, this was not a new tactic for the government, but was simply taken to a new level after 1987. The key here is that, in many ways, the government forces were more thorough in their demolition of Kurdish villages than they were in the murder of the inhabitants. Although they killed people on a scale that is hard to believe, they were also prepared to capture and detain people. Villages, however, were destroyed utterly, down to the last building.

Why was this? I would suggest that it is because Saddam's regime was aware that the destruction of my people did not *require* the immediate murder of every last Kurd. It did, however, require the destruction of our way of life, the destruction of our ability to rebuild, and the destruction of our ability to fight back in future if the regime moved to complete its campaign of murder.

The destruction of villages was crucial in that. The Iraqi army would have known from years of fighting peshmerga that it could not hope to kill or capture every Kurd in an area. Leaving villages intact, therefore, would have allowed them to rebuild. More than that, it would have left resources for anyone hiding to use to affect a more permanent escape.

It also served to destroy the essentially rural life of the Kurdish people, to such an extent that even today, more than ninety percent of the population is urban. That was certainly delib-erate, because a rural Kurdish population was much harder to regulate and control. Again, it seems like the regime accepted that it could not immediately kill all of my people, but *was* creating the conditions in which it could do so in future.

With an emphasis even in the Anfal on captur-ing my people, what happened to the tens of thousands of people taken in it? The answer is that many of those captured *were* killed. Some were executed immediately, under the laws governing the prohibited zones where their own villages stood. Others were killed after initial processing by the army. In area after area, men were separated from women and taken away, never to be seen again. From what happened in 1983, we can only assume that they were systematically killed, probably in the desert.

Most of the remaining men, women and children were taken to the 'camps' described above. Camps that make even the one I and my family were taken to look comfortable by comparison. In many, people were starved to death, beaten and tortured, but that was not the worst fate for some of them. Again and again there are stories of Kurdish women being raped or trafficked into effective slavery, usually in the south of the country, as far away from their families, homes and hopes of escape as possible.

I have stayed away from one figure until this point. 182,000 people. That is, as far as we can tell, the number of my people killed by Saddam's regime overall. Up to a hundred thousand of them died during the period 1987-8.[12] I have stayed away from the total figure until now, because the sheer enormity of it can sometimes make the rest of what happened hard to take in.

That figure is, of course, not a precise one. It is based largely on people who cannot be accounted for, or who are known to have been killed thanks to the regime's insistence on keeping records of its operations. As such, there is plenty of scope for people to argue with it,

12   *Genocide in Iraq: The Anfal Campaign Against the Kurds*, (Human Rights Watch, New York, 1993 and 2006)

as Ali Hassan Al-Majid did in his trial when he claimed that his forces had killed "only" fifty thousand Kurds. Fifty thousand Kurds would still be a huge, unforgivable number, but it is nowhere near the truth. Even the hundred thousand claimed as the official statistic does not take account of the misery inflicted on those imprisoned, taken from their homes, or even simply forced to flee as refugees to Iran. Were we to include those numbers in the total, we might be faced with figures past the million mark.

We are certainly talking about a series of events that dramatically changed Kurdistan. The Anfal changed the lives of its people. It proved once and for all that Saddam and many of those around him were genuinely interested in destroying my people, rather than simply in maintaining control of the country. It wiped out, not just many of the people from villages, but whole identities, as people lost the places they had come from, their families, even the use of their language.

Yet despite all this, it seems to be one event in the whole campaign that people are drawn to. Again and again, the horrors of the Anfal, the repression that preceded it, are just seen as secondary to one key event. That event is the bombing of Halabja, and the murder of up to five thousand people using chemical weapons.

Why is that? What role did it actually play in the Anfal? Should earlier events be seen as being at least as significant? Those are the questions we must now go on to ask.

5

Halabja

The events of Halabja have probably received more attention than the rest of the atrocities committed against the Kurds by Saddam's forces. There are understandable reasons for this, as we will discuss below, but sometimes the focus can obscure events that claimed far more lives. Nevertheless, it is important to understand Halabja, because it serves as a symbol of Saddam's approach to my people, because it allows us to explore the tactics of propaganda used by the regime around its atrocities, and because, even though there were other equally important moments of violence, the bombing of Halabja did claim some 3,000-5,000 lives.

Why has there been a focus on it? Why have previous books made it their central element, as Hiltermann does[13], rather than just one incident in a sustained campaign against my people? Part of the answer undoubtedly lies in the stated presence of weapons of mass destruction as a justification for the Western invasion of Iraq. In ostensibly examining Halabja, writers such as Hiltermann actually examine a much broader

13   Hiltermann, *Halabja: A Poisonous Affair*

range of questions relating to chemical weapons and international attitudes to them. There is nothing wrong with that, but it does move the emphasis away from my people, and so creates a book with very different aims to this one.

Another part may come down to simple self-interest. For many outsiders, the genocide of the Kurds is simply something that happened a long way away. It does not affect them, or if it does, it does so only in a general way. The use of chemical weapons against civilian targets, however, is an issue that has the potential to affect anyone, anywhere. So is potential complicity in shifting the blame for the events, which is the issue that Hiltermann focuses on.

For some writers, Halabja may also have been chosen because the full scope of the suffering of my people under Saddam is difficult to take in, and that is more understandable. Sometimes, people need a symbol because they cannot cope with the full reality of something, and Halabja certainly works as that. The danger comes when the symbol starts to be seen as the whole reality, and 3,000-5,000 deaths start to be taken as a substitute for 182,000. In too many books, the Anfal and all the previous attacks on my people are given just a chapter or so as background to this one massacre, when really it should be the other way around.

So I have tried to avoid focussing too much

on the events of Halabja elsewhere in this book. The regime's efforts at genocide did not start or end there. Their hatred of the Kurds did not find its expression solely in that city, and their tactics were not defined solely by those they used there. Indeed, in the last chapter, I suggested that their most effective tactics against my people came when they sought to use chemical attacks only in conjunction with other methods. That is a theme I will explore more here.

Nevertheless, Halabja does warrant at least some serious attention. It represented one of the earliest attacks in the Anfal campaign, coming on the 16th of March 1988, and so helps to show the point where Saddam's troops moved to the outright slaughter of my people (though remember that the preparatory phase of the Anfal had already killed or displaced many). It remains the highest number of casualties due to chemical weapons use anywhere, and a major breach of international conventions. It is one of the few times in the Anfal that the regime attacked a city directly. It also demonstrates a lot about the propaganda machine of the Iraqi government of the time, and about the willingness of Saddam's international friends to aid him. All of those are important issues.

Let's start with the background to what happened. We already know from the previous chapter that under Ali Hassan Al-Majid there

must have been plans put in place to attack
the Kurds over the period from 1987. It seems
likely, therefore, that the regime was simply
looking for an appropriate opportunity to put
them into action. At the start of March 1988, that
excuse came along. At what was the height of
the Iran-Iraq war, in response to Iraqi missile
attacks, the Iranian military moved into the
north of Iraq, with aid from peshmerga. At some
point prior to the 16th of March, they succeeded
in moving into the city of Halabja, though there
is little evidence that they stayed there.

The brief facts of what happened next are as
follows. On the 16th of March, the Iraqi military
bombed the city with chemical weapons
dropped from planes. It preceded the bombing
with scouting from helicopters, both to recon-
noitre the area and to check wind direction. The
overwhelming majority of fatalities and casualties resulting from that attack came in the form
of civilians, not Iranian troops or peshmerga.
The numbers of dead are estimated at between
three and five thousand, while anywhere up to
ten thousand may have been injured, though
both of these figures are difficult to prove with
any certainty.

Put like that, it sounds so simple, yet there
are many questions that need to be asked about
the events of that day, about its aftermath, and
about its place within the regime's campaign of

destruction as a whole. Let's start with some of the key details of the attack, the regime's actions, and the civilian responses to it.

First, let's be clear about one thing: this was a deliberate attack on a civilian target, aimed at killing as many Kurds as possible. That can be seen both in the targeting of the city, when any peshmerga were outside it, and in the choice of weapons. Why use chemical weapons in a city if the intention were to attack military forces? Just as importantly, any Iranian forces left in the city would have been more than capable of dealing with a chemical attack, so it was really only civilians at risk. Combine that with the use of chemical weapons against civilian targets throughout the rest of the Anfal, and it is easy to see that this was not a military attack with civilian collateral damage, this was an attack always intended to kill at least as many civilians as peshmerga or Iranian troops.

That is important, because there have been writers who have treated Halabja as something separate from the Anfal that it sat within. It has occasionally been treated as a legitimate military offensive using illegitimate means (chemical weapons) rather than as a part of a more general genocide against the Kurds.

This, I feel, is both not an accurate reflection of the attack on Halabja, and a misunderstanding of the nature of the Anfal as a whole. The Anfal was a genocide that killed tens of thousands of civilians, yet the regime always claimed it was acting against rebels, dissidents and peshmerga. There was, throughout, a confusion of the military and the civil, a targeting of civilians while claiming military aims. *That* fits with Halabja, even if some aspects, such as the targeting of a city rather than a rural area, seem anomalous. Trying to split an attack off from the Anfal because of potential military targets in the area simply does not work.

That the Iraqi military knew that they would be primarily targeting civilians is hard to doubt. For one thing, Halabja was a city, not easily evacuated and certainly not likely to be free from civilian targets. For another, there are the reports of helicopters scouting the area, so the military commanders ordering the attack would have been aware throughout, not just that there was a risk of civilian casualties, but the precise extent of the civilian presence in the city. They would also have known that any military targets were outside the city, not within it.

The chemical weapons used seem to have been dropped from Iraqi MIGs. This is a tactic used in some phases of the Anfal but not in others, when artillery was used to deliver the weapons instead. Is this difference a meaningful one? Was it dictated by the nature of the target, or by other considerations? My guess is that the urban target probably played a role in the choice of delivery method, since an airborne attack may have been simply easier in such circumstances. Yet there may also have been other factors at play.

Consider those occasions when we know that artillery mounted chemical weapons were used during the Anfal. In general, they were used as part of other tactics, driving people towards ground forces as they fled. The use of aircraft in Halabja suggests a more isolated attack, and certainly there seems to have been no attempt at the kind of secondary ground operation used elsewhere. That combination suggests the use of chemical weapons to kill as many people as possible directly. It also suggests, again, that there was no focus on defeating another military force.

We know from accounts from the city that the initial reaction to the attacks was one of surprise. People huddled in cellars, basements and bomb shelters, believing that the city was about to be shelled or bombarded with conventional weapons. It is a sad reflection on the frequency with which my people have been caught up in the middle of other people's wars that the inhabitants of the city were so ready for that kind of conventional attack.

They were not prepared for bombs that did not explode, and we have many accounts of people not believing that something else was happening until it was too late. Survivors consistently say that there was the smell of sulphur, but most only linked that to the idea of chemical weapons once they or people around them began to display symptoms.

Those symptoms included a wide range of complaints, including blackening of the skin, eye irritation, confusion, lack of coordination, inability to breathe and more. They are not fully explained by a single poison, suggesting that a combination of different chemical weapons was used in the attack. Commentators have suggested that the combination may have included elements such as mustard gas and cyanide, among others.

Whatever the combination was, it was heavier than air. That meant that those civilians who had taken shelter from potential shelling were the ones most at risk in the attack. They stayed there because they believed they would be safe, and there are stories of people trying to keep their families there to protect them, not understanding the full extent of the danger. The ones who stayed in their shelters died.

So did many of those who attempted to escape. People made for the river, thinking that it would disperse the gas, or simply attempted to escape Halabja any other way they could. Many did not make it. There are stories of people becoming separated from their families and quickly being lost. Since confusion was one of the symptoms of the gas, that contributed to the number of those breaking away from safety or going in the wrong direction. It is hard to see how any of those doing so could have survived.

I have said before that it is hard to know precisely how many people died, and even harder to know how many were injured in the attack. We don't know, for example, how many people have died from longer term effects brought on by exposure to the gas, and mustard gas is notorious for its long term effects. Nor, in a region where so many people have been shifted away from their homes and so many more were killed later in the Anfal, can we simply take the number of people missing from around the area as an indication of those killed in the attack.

So there are serious limitations when it comes to judging the extent of the casualties from the attacks, but there are also some sources of information, such as medical reports and accounts from immediately afterwards. The consensus as I stated at the start of the chapter, seems to be that at least three thousand people were killed in Halabja, and possibly as many as five thousand. Up to twice that number may have been injured as a result of coming into contact with toxic chemicals.

I have briefly explored the kinds of injuries

that were inflicted by the attack above, but two points go on to add to their seriousness. The first is the lack of immediate medical attention for most of the inhabitants. There are stories of people who were able to secure shots of atropine from the local medical centre, or who were able to get medical attention from those peshmerga close to the city. In both cases though, getting help meant being able to travel to it, and many of the worst affected simply couldn't do so.

Even where they could get some medical attention, it must often have been basic. We are limited in what we can know here, because most of the stories that come to us of the injured are from those who *were* able to get to more complete medical facilities, but we know from those stories that often, measures such as intubation or tracheotomies were necessary to assist breathing, sometimes accompanied by the debridement of dead tissue or the use of significant amounts of fluids to stabilise the injured.

I can, therefore, only imagine what things must have been like for those injured but unable to get to immediate medical help. How many must have died trying to escape over the border into Iran, or deep into the mountains? How many people must have realised the severity of their symptoms too late? Even from survivors, we hear stories of other people trapped with them, who were weaker, or who simply got a larger dose of the gas. Often, even in stories from those shelters where people were able to escape, those stories start with individuals who started to exhibit symptoms in the minutes after the attack, as the 'wrong' smell started to seep in, and who died before anyone could help them.

A second point, and one of the cruellest elements of the attack on Halabja, was that often, it was the very young or the very old who succumbed. Where previous atrocities such as the mass murder of 1983 at least made a pretence of targeting only those men who could fight back, the chemical weapons used on Halabja were *least* likely to kill the young and strong, because those were the ones who could survive the largest doses of the gas, who could flee fastest in the face of it, and who were probably least dependant on others for their escape. Indeed, because many of Kurdistan's men would have been either peshmerga or already fleeing the regime's cruelty, it is likely that there were fewer of them in the city than other, more vulnerable groups. Certainly, those sheltering in basements were much more likely to be women, children, or the elderly.

Would the attacking forces have known this? As with the general danger to civilians, I believe that they must have. They would have known the effects of their weapons without a doubt, from earlier uses dating back to at least the mid-1980s. In any case, it is simply common sense that strong young men are less likely to be vulnerable to most toxins. They must also have known from their on-going war with Iran how the inhabitants would probably react in the event of bombardment. Coupled with their initial helicopter based scouting, it seems hard to believe that they could not have worked out who would have been most at risk from the gas.

What happened in the aftermath of the attack? The more limited follow up operation compared with the third Anfal in particular was one characteristic of the attack on Halabja. That seems to have meant that, once beyond the effects of the initial gas attack, those able to get away that far were able to make a fuller escape, generally to Iran. Perhaps there were some who were captured by the Iraqi military in the follow up to the attack, but the relative lack of accounts from those captured under those circumstances seems to suggest otherwise. At best, it suggests that people were able to escape the area of the city and simply have not come forward, which makes sense, given the presence of the peshmerga nearby. At worst, it suggests that the military killed anyone it found, which would be consistent with both the idea of the prohibited zones and the campaign of disinformation that followed.

It is at this point that I am able to comment directly on Halabja, because although I was not there, and I was still in the camp at this point, I *did* get to hear about it. We all did, and crucially, what we heard was the regime's official version of events. At the core of that version was the suggestion that Iran had bombed Halabja with chemical weapons, and it was so successful that until as late as 1993, despite everything the regime had done to me and my family, I was willing to believe it.

Why was that? How did Saddam's propaganda machine succeed in convincing the world, even temporarily, that his forces were not behind the Halabja attack? How did it succeed in convincing his own people; even many of *my* people? When it comes to Halabja, understanding the aftermath is crucial to getting a grip on the way the regime mixed violence with propaganda.

There was one clever move the regime made in that aftermath: it didn't try to deny what had happened. If it had done that, then it would have been clear relatively quickly that it was trying to protect itself from the consequences of using chemical weapons on its own people. It understood that pretending Halabja hadn't happened was impossible, since as early as April, a UN medical examiner was dispatched to gather evidence of injuries and produce a report. That report was repetitive in its listing of severe chemical injuries and left no doubt about the use of chemical weapons in the city. There was no room for Saddam's regime to simply deny what had happened.

Instead, it sought to twist opinion, blaming the other side of the conflict in which Halabja found itself caught up, and doing that surprisingly cleverly. It was not a case of a flat denial, or even a straightforward accusation. Instead, Saddam's regime seems to have simply spent its time pointing out occasions on which Iran had used chemical weapons, planting the seed of the idea.

Elements in the US seem to have helped with that obfuscation, either unknowingly, or because they wanted to shift pressure onto Tehran. The US State Department and the Regan administration in general actually appear to have been behind some of the worst confusion over the aftermath, possibly in an attempt to prevent a UN resolution against what it saw as an ally in the Middle East.

Some of that was subtle, dropping hints and asking for more details of *Iran's* involvement in chemical weapons. Asking rather than asserting it made it seem obvious that Iran had done *something*. It made it seem like something everybody knew, about which America only wanted a few more facts. It made others go around looking for those facts, and persuaded them to treat any vague hints that they found as proof of what the US had already told them that they 'knew'. As a piece of statecraft, it was very clever. As an action in the aftermath of a major chemical attack, it was cold and amoral.

US state department guidelines on the issue make it clear that the US government wanted to persuade those around it that Iran was at least partly to blame.[14] The guidelines cited evidence that the Secretary of State apparently had but couldn't show anyone that Iran was involved. It was a way to start a rumour, and more than that. It was a bald statement of the US government's position on the attacks; a position that said that Iran had to take at least some of the blame for any use of chemical weapons in the city.

What was that statement based on? It is likely that we will never know. It is possible that Saddam's regime was able to persuade the US that it knew something they didn't about the events in the city. It is possible that the US Secretary of State genuinely believed that there *was* evidence of Iran's complicity. It is also possible that it was entirely made up to support a UN position on Iran and Iraq that was in the USA's favour. What is certain now though is that Iran was not involved, though it took me

---

14   Quoted in Hiltermann pp126-7

more than five years to be convinced of that. It perhaps saves me a little embarrassment to note that the UN was just as convinced, because the resolution it issued in the wake of the attack instructed both Iraq *and* Iran to refrain from any future chemical weapons use.

Why? Why did people believe the lie rather than the truth? Why did the UN, the people of Iraq, my people, and countries all around the world all believe that Halabja was down to someone other than Saddam? I will be looking more closely at general reasons why they ignored the wider genocide in a later chapter, but there *are* reasons that are specific to Halabja. The role of the US is one, and probably the main one, since people were more inclined to believe what the US said than anything Saddam did. After all, we were told, the US had one of the best intelligence services in the world, and an abiding interest in freedom. If they didn't tell the truth about something like this, who would?

Yet there were other factors. The fact that it came relatively early in the Anfal campaign was probably a part of it. Had it come in September 1988, after months of chemical attacks, it might have been clear that the Iraqi regime was the sole author of the events of that day. As it was, it represented a break with the lower level tactics of village clearance and arbitrary imprisonment used by Saddam's followers, making it easier to believe that it could have been done by someone else. Coming at the start of the campaign, in circumstances seeming to implicate the Iranians, it seemed almost like the use of chemical weapons in the rest of the Anfal was *copying* those tactics from someone else, rather than simply repeating them.

The fact that Halabja was a town probably contributed to that. Indeed, it remains a key piece of evidence for anyone still convinced that the attack did not truly form part of the Anfal, but was something separate.

The Anfal, as people generally envision it, was an attack on rural Kurdistan. An attack on a city seems like something else at first glance.

It probably also helped the lie that the Iranians, or at least Iranian sponsored peshmerga, *had* attacked government forces in the city.

On the 16th, the very day the attack happened, Iran announced that it had 'liberated' Halabja.

That announcement probably related to military actions taking place in the two or three days before that, and again, I would like to emphasise that peshmerga forces were mostly outside the city by the 16th, but the timing of that announcement certainly made it *sound* like Iranian forces were still engaged in military action around Halabja on that date.There were unconfirmed reports of chemical weapons use by both sides earlier in the war, too. Whether there was any truth to them is impossible to say, but maybe that is the point. The sporadic use of chemical weapons was something that was very hard to disprove, and in turn, the rumours seemed to support the bigger lie.

Finally, there is the simple point that people *wanted* it to be true. Partly, because Iran had attacked us nearly as much as Saddam over the years. Partly, because it seemed inconceivable that anyone, even Saddam, would do something like this to his own people. Mostly though, I think that my people wanted to believe it because they knew that if the Iranians hadn't done it, then the Iraqi government was finally taking action to murder us en masse. A one off Iranian attack was a less terrifying option than the first step of a sustained programme of genocide, even if the rest of the Anfal proved exactly who had been behind it.

I want to look now at where the chemical attack on Halabja fit into the regime's broader programme. How does it fit into the Anfal? How does it fit into the persecution of my people within Iraq as a whole? Can we do anything to explain the anomaly of an attack on a city? Does Halabja deserve its special place in the minds of those commenting on Saddam's repression of the Kurds?

Probably the most important point here, and the one I have been trying to emphasise throughout this chapter, is that Halabja did not represent a special or one off event. It *was* a part of the Anfal campaign, despite attempts by the Iraqi government to shift the blame or portray it as an essentially military event. More than that, it was a very early part of the Anfal, which makes Halabja interesting both in terms of the ways future attacks on my people copied it and in the ways that they deviated from the model it provided. In some ways, we can almost see the events of Halabja as part of a 'trial run' for the rest of the Anfal, using the excuse of a carefully provoked Iranian incursion to test the viability of chemical weapons attacks within Kurdistan.

The use of chemical weapons continued throughout the Anfal. In that much, Halabja can be seen as a 'successful' trial for Saddam's government. Another element that continued was the use of aircraft to drop chemical weapons in several phases of the Anfal. In some, again, there seems to have been an emphasis on using the weapons primarily to kill, and little focus on capturing those fleeing. Judging by accounts of injuries from those who survived later attacks, the types of chemical weapons employed seem to have remained the same as well.

In other ways, things changed. While there were phases of the Anfal that were very similar to Halabja, there were also phases where artillery was used as the primary means of delivery, and where chemical weapons seem to have been used primarily as a tool to force people out of their villages for capture or execution. The campaign on the Germian plain in particular seems not to have matched Halabja's tactics. Then there is the recurring issue of Halabja being an urban target, rather than a village.

If we see Halabja as almost an experiment by the government with new tactics, then these variations become less difficult to understand. The changes cease to be evidence of Halabja's separation from the rest of the Anfal, and instead become simply adaptations made as the genocidal campaign progressed. Adaptations made to overcome what Saddam and his supporters would probably have seen as weaknesses of the attack on Halabja, because despite the very high numbers of casualties, they still mean that less than a seventh of the city's population was injured by the gas. Seen in that way, the tactical changes made over the course of the Anfal simply demonstrate quite clearly the regime's desire to kill a higher proportion of my people.

The focus on more rural targets for the rest of the Anfal, meanwhile, can be explained in one of a number of ways, each of which may have had some influence on the decision. The first is the uproar that Halabja created. As a densely packed urban centre with good communications, it was in the international eye enough that attacking it created immediate repercussions. Those were only avoided by shifting the blame onto Iran; a tactic that probably could not have been repeated easily. As such, the regime may have felt that another such urban use of chemical weapons would have been hard to get away with in the short term, forcing it to concentrate on more rural targets.

Secondly, the Iranian 'liberation' of Halabja provided the regime with the excuse it needed for its actions, but such excuses would have been difficult to come by for other cities. Villages could be uprooted, because that had always been a traditional tactic in Iraq against the Kurds, but another assault on a town would have been hard to justify without an additional 'excuse' of the same type.

Thirdly, there is the increasing Arabisation of Kurdistan under Saddam's regime. That introduction of Arab families was particularly the case in and around key urban centres, which the regime would have seen as crucial to the control of their regions. While the regime could destroy villages utterly, using chemical weapons within one of Kurdistan's other cities would have actually worked *against* the government's desire for greater control over the area, both by damaging cities it needed for that control, and by killing Arab families loyal to it.

Finally, there is one more possibility, which must have been at least a consideration. That possibility is that attacking another urban centre would have been far more effective once people had been driven to it by the Anfal in the countryside. I have already written that I believe it was Saddam's long term goal to eradicate my people, and that I think the regime would have repeated its actions of 1983 in the1990s and beyond.

Although this can be no more than speculation, perhaps Halabja was a vision of the methods Saddam intended to use to accomplish those aims. Perhaps the Anfals were to round up my people, and then eventually, probably the next time Iraq went to war with Iran if history is any guide, the plan was to use chemical weapons against the camps.

As with other aspects of Saddam's intentions, we will thankfully never know, yet I think we know more about Halabja if we see it in the context of the rest of the Anfal, and in the context of a much longer campaign against my people.

It was a terrible event, but if we do not see it as simply one point within the wider violence, it runs the risk of obscuring the other atrocities of the regime.

Worse, I think it is impossible to fully under-stand Halabja that way. It must be seen as something more than a one off atrocity. It must be seen as a trial run for what came next, and possibly, just possibly, as a glimpse of the future Saddam had in mind for all Kurds.

6

1991 uprising

After the Anfal, we had to go back to waiting. Stuck in the camps, we didn't get any other choice. We knew some of what had been happening, but not all of it. Perhaps if we had known the full extent of the things the Iraqi regime had been doing to my people, we would have been more frightened, but perhaps not. After all, we heard enough of what was happening to know that worse could be coming for us, but what could we do except wait?

It is possible that the Anfal would have been followed by worse atrocities against my people. That certainly seems to be consistent with what we know of Saddam Hussein, and of his regime. It is possible that the intention was to follow up those massacres with more once my people were sufficiently concentrated in camps to allow for it, or once it seemed that our usefulness to the regime was at an end.

Because in this period, it became clear that we were a resource for the regime as much as something to be destroyed. That had always been true to some extent: our men had always been taken for the Iraqi army, while our women and children were used as hostages to try to bring in peshmerga from the mountains, or simply sold off into slavery. The events of the mid-1980s, however, seemed to accelerate that process, and introduced new pressures.

There had always been pressures on families to hand over their peshmerga members, for example, but in this period, there were so many people taken as prisoners that there was almost an industry of intimidation, with the army coming in more and more to try to pressure us into handing them over. They felt that if we only sent messages to them, they would come running down from the mountains, ready to be killed.

There was also our role as human shields to consider in this period. To some extent, it had always been true, and certainly women and children were pushed ahead of government forces in the more conventional (i.e. not chemical weapon led) elements of the Anfal. Yet it is in this period, with the construction of more and more new camps, that their locations came to be at least partly about protecting the military bases near them. After all, what enemy would risk bombing military installations if it also meant killing Kurdish civilians?

Actually, one answer to that explains why it may have become more important in this period. The Americans wouldn't. The Iranians, the Turks, and the other countries in the region in occasional conflict with Iraq probably *would* have, unless using peshmerga to fight their battles for them. The Americans, with more of an awareness of their public image, had to be more careful.

That came to matter in the period after 1988, because it was a phase of increasing tension between Iraq and the USA that eventually led to the First Gulf War of 1990-1991. That build-up of international tension might not sound important, given that I and my family were in a camp, while so many more of our people were dead or over the border in Iran. It might sound too far removed from us to have had an effect on our lives, yet I want to argue here that it actually potentially affected us a great deal.

As I have suggested above, it made us useful human shields around Iraqi military installations, at least until the Americans showed that they were able to bomb much more precisely than Saddam's military thought. But the build-up of tension did more than that. It created a situation in which Saddam could not advance any plan for our extermination, for fear of the consequences it might involve.

That is one area where the regime was always very clever. It knew how far it could push without incurring international action. It had pushed exactly that far in 1988, going to the extent that a UN resolution was passed against its use of chemical weapons (albeit diluted by including an injunction against Iran using them too). The breakdown of diplomatic relations between Iraq and the USA meant that, for a while, at least, Saddam couldn't risk giving them an excuse for war by finishing what he had started with us.

There is also a simple question of attention here. While it seems likely that Saddam and some of those closest to him wanted the Kurds destroyed, many more seem to have been focussed on doing just enough to keep us in our 'place'. On making sure that we, or rather the peshmerga, couldn't be a problem for the regime. That is why the moments of the greatest atrocities against my people have coincided either with uprisings or with wars against Iran, where Iraq couldn't risk a simultaneous uprising.

In the aftermath of the Anfal, there probably did not seem to be a risk of such an uprising. My people were, for the moment at least, contained, exiled, or dead. As such, when other threats to the regime came into view, those inevitably took the attention of the military. They simply did not have the time to mount another campaign on the scale of the Anfal, nor would they have been able to do it without leaving themselves militarily very open.

We must also remember that the destruction of my people was not the regime's only military objective. It seems obvious looking back that in the period 1988-1990, Saddam's generals must have been planning the invasion of Kuwait that came in August 1990 and sparked the First Gulf War. Indeed, that invasion provides another avenue of exploration when it comes to the Anfal, because an awareness of those future objectives must have had at least some influence on the regime's desire to deal with my people at home first.

Indeed, I could go further there and suggest that part of the reason Saddam's men did not proceed further with the destruction of my people in the period 1989-1990 may have been down to that need to prepare for the coming invasion. Perhaps they wanted to produce a stable environment in Iraq to allow for that invasion, an environment that would not be provided by an on-going campaign designed to kill my people, or by the diplomatic fall out it would cause.

Whatever the reason, in the three years following the Anfal, the final burst of mass murder we feared did not come. Not even once war started with Coalition forces in 1990, which stands in stark contrast to the way the regime acted in response to its wars with Iran. What does that say about the intentions of the regime?

Perhaps it simply says that it did not fear peshmerga at the time, since they did not have the same alliance with the Coalition at that stage that they did with Iran.

Perhaps though, it also shows the extent to which the regime was caught up in the First Gulf War. Even the architect of much of the Anfal, Ali Hassan Al Majid, was called away to serve as military governor for Kuwait. Perhaps his absence contributed to the regime's failure to pursue its previous policies of violence towards my people during the war.

It wasn't caught up in it for long, though. Foreign military intervention began in a largely defensive capacity in August 1990, moved to a more aggressive operation in January 1991, and was done by February of that year. Suddenly, my people were faced with Iraq in the aftermath of a war where the regime had fared badly, where they would be looking for someone to blame, and where Saddam now had his military to call upon again, rather than it being caught up in fighting over Kuwait. Even Al Majid was back.

Looked at like that, it is easy to see how things could have been different. If we had sat and waited in the camps, if we hadn't dared to do anything, my people could so easily have been treated as scapegoats once again, targeted for the 'crime' of the regime being under pressure. Saddam could so easily have decided that, with the war done, he was in as good a position as he ever would be to start killing my people en masse once again. If we had stayed in the camps, we could have been wiped out as his troops finished the violence that Saddam's troubles elsewhere in the Middle East had deferred. I do not know for certain that they would have done so, of course. It is possible that we might have been left in the camps and ignored, though that is not consistent with the regime's responses previously.

I do know two things. The first is that the Coalition forces do not seem to have taken all this into account when they stopped their war, or if they did, then they decided that the lives of Kurdish men, women and children were not worth the lives of their soldiers to defend. They called a halt to the war, apparently heedless of the backlash that could have come our way. Worse, seeming to know how bad it could be, because what the Americans did next would not have come if they did not have at least an inkling of what might happen.

Secondly, I know that we do not have to worry about what might have happened had we stayed in the camps, because in 1991, my people rose up to free themselves. How much bravery must it have taken to do that? So many times, rising up had led to yet another wave of repression, doing no more than costing the lives of my people, yet in 1991, they were prepared to try again.

Why? Part of it must be the simple refusal of the Kurds to give in. The same refusal that had Saddam and his regime treating us as something to be wiped out meant in 1991 that despite the tens of thousands dead in the years before that, peshmerga were still prepared to do what was necessary to protect their people. Indeed, perhaps that played a part, showing the peshmerga what would happen to their friends and family if they did not act.

Yet clearly that was not the whole reason. If it were, then the uprising would have happened before 1991. Much more of it, I suspect, was down to the combination of the end of the First Gulf War and the rise of the Marsh-Arabs in the south. The end of the war showed the peshmerga that foreign powers were not going to do the job of helping their people, meaning that they would have to do it themselves, and quickly if they wanted to succeed. The US president, George Bush, even said as much in late February, calling on the people of Iraq to rise up against Saddam, presumably in the knowledge that US forces would not be doing the job of removing him at that time.

Circumstances helped, of course. The rising of the Marsh-Arabs in the south may have been the opportunity my people were waiting for, certainly when combined with the ban on fixed wing aircraft in the northern no-fly zone. The limitations on Saddam's air forces, coupled with the distraction of his ground forces, meant that my people were finally in a position to take what was theirs, and to free those taken by the regime.

My key memory of the uprising comes in the form of my brother. I had not seen him since we went into the camp. I thought he was dead. My mother had kept the fact that he was alive from us, to protect both him and us since he was fighting as a peshmerga in the mountains. I remember waking up in the night at the start of March 1991 to hear people moving around in our house in the camp. I went to see what was going on.

I found my mother in the kitchen, talking to a man I did not know, who was dressed as a peshmerga. It was obvious that something was happening. I could practically feel the excitement and tension there as I walked in. Yet when I asked what was going on and who this man was, my mother told me to go back to bed and forget it. I refused, asking again.

It was then that my mother told me that this was my brother. I refused to believe it. My brother was dead. She'd told me so herself. It took probably another five or ten minutes before I would even believe that much, and then I was so happy at the thought of having a brother alive whom I had thought was dead that I barely remembered how things had been when I walked in. For a short time, I was too busy hearing about how he had escaped to Iran with my uncle, and what things had been like for him as a peshmerga. It was only later that I thought to ask what was happening, and why he was in the camp now.

He told us something that seemed impossible. He told us that the peshmerga would be taking the camp in the morning, and that we should be ready to leave. Around Kurdistan, families must have been having similar conversations with their peshmerga members, because what happened next was far more than just the taking of a single camp.

The rebellion in the south began around three days before my people were able to rise up in the north, yet the speed with which my people acted more than made up for it. Rania was the first town where the inhabitants rose up, but virtually all the others in the north quickly followed. In less than two weeks, practically every town in Kurdistan had fallen to peshmerga, the prisoners in the camps around them being set free, government documents on everything from the Anfal to the day to day oppression of my people being seized before they could be destroyed. Even Kirkuk, the city that the Bagdad regime had tried so hard to Arabise, fell by the 20th of March.

How did the revolt proceed so quickly? Part of it was the sheer depth of popular feeling against Saddam. After more than a decade of oppression under his regime, the vast majority of people in Kurdistan, even the majority of people in much of Iraq as a whole, were ready to be rid of him. More than that, it seems likely that they believed that it was finally possible in a way that it would not have been just a few years before. The radio exhortations to rise up may have created the impression that if they could only revolt, they would receive at least some support from the US.

Whatever the truth of that, the level of organisation in the revolution was probably a big factor in its speed. Remember, by this point, my people had been fighting against the regime in some form for decades, and peshmerga had done so in the context of several wars, including those against Iran. The peshmerga had defined command structures, while the two main parties, the PDK (generally called the KDP by Western sources) and the PUK, had established chains of command waiting in exile outside Iraq. The PDK in particular had the authority and organisational structure to be able to move quickly in a situation that demanded action.

As such, although the image of a popular

uprising is true in many respects, in other crucial ones it falls short of the mark. Yes, the cause of the uprising was a popular one in Kurdistan, and yes, there was popular support, but the bulk of the uprising was fuelled by returning and battle hardened peshmerga fighters, used to taking on the regime. The revolt proceeded swiftly because it was a well organised event conducted by expert fighters with decent weaponry, far removed from any images that might be conjured up of ordinary people fighting back with whatever they had to hand.

It is hard to underestimate the importance of leadership in 1991. Massoud Barzani and the Barzani family in general were at the heart of the revolt, coming back from exile in Iran to help organise large portions of it. Of course, with such a widespread revolt, there were multiple centres for it and multiple groups trying to claim control, but temporarily at least, the different groups within the peshmerga were able to put aside enough of their differences to create what my people had been looking for almost since the creation of Iraq: a separate Kurdistan.

It is important to consider another factor here, in the form of the lack of opposition. We have already seen that the regime was able and willing to murder my people in their tens of thousands, so there can be no doubt that had it been prepared for a popular uprising in the north, it would have acted brutally. Indeed, it did so in the south, slaughtering at least 50,000-60,000 people there. Yet with so many troops called away the peshmerga in the north were able to take whole cities with just minimal opposition. Often, they were able to take camps before the guards even knew what was happening.

At its height, the uprising must have terrified Saddam and his followers. Just four of Iraq's provinces, and none of those in the north, remained firmly in government hands by the end of March. Indeed, the extent to which the uprising scared the regime may be seen in its attempt to offer terms for a ceasefire to both my people in the north and to rebels further south. It probably seemed like a clever move to Saddam, trying to get his enemies to slacken in their fighting long enough to attack them.

All of those he offered terms to saw through them, yet somehow, despite that, the would-be revolution failed. By the end of April, Saddam was firmly back in control of Iraq, and we had to run. How did that happen? How did my people's big chance to be free turn into a situation where we had to flee for our lives?

Part of it was the success of the regime's efforts in the south.

The army leaving to focus on that rebellion allowed Kurdistan a chance to rise up in revolt, but it also meant that it was able to bring its full weight to bear on the rebellion in the south. The regime was quick to employ many of the tactics it had used previously in Kurdistan and elsewhere, from mass village clearances to arbitrary arrests and murder, and although it stopped short of the prolonged use of chemical weapons employed against my people, it was still sufficient to derail that rebellion.

There was the transient desire to be on the winning side to consider as well. With so many areas rising up in revolt against the regime, it seems likely to me that at least some were doing so because they did not want to be seen as supporting Saddam in the aftermath. That, or they rose up because it seemed that they would succeed and they wanted a role in determining Iraq's political future. They did not have the same history of conflict with the regime that the Kurds did, but instead rose up only so long as it looked like they might win.

There was an inequality of weaponry to consider. The rebels had organisation and desire to win, but generally even the peshmerga had only light weaponry, supplemented by occasional RPGs. That combination was good for guerrilla warfare in the mountains, and even for the kind of sudden strikes needed to take locations, but it was less useful when it came to *holding* those locations against armoured divisions or helicopter gunships. The rebels on both sides could win a lightning war, but not a grinding one.

There was the point where it became clear there would be no outside help, too. The call from George Bush to rise up might have seemed to have contained the implicit assurance that the US would be behind any uprising, but instead, it was the US calling on the people of Iraq to do what it was not prepared to. It sought to use them the way so many countries have tried to use Kurdistan in the past, as a proxy to fight wars while 'only' losing Kurdish lives. Once it became clear that there would be no help coming, that must have cost the uprising some of its momentum.

Momentum was crucial, because although the uprising in the north was generally well organised through the main Kurdish political parties and the peshmergas' command structure, it was not directly connected to the uprisings elsewhere. So, instead of one, or even two uprisings able to support one another, what we had were many separate uprisings, each one a powerful contributing factor when they all happened together, but each one small enough that it could be crushed if the regime focussed enough forces on it. All Saddam and his cronies had to do was hold on long enough and hope that they could chip away at enough of the revolts to turn the tide back in their favour.

Just as the revolt in the south began before
the one in Kurdistan, so too it finished earlier.
Before the start of April, the regime use of shelling, mass arrests and helicopter attacks had
taken back every southern city gained during
the uprising. That effectively freed the military
to come back north, and while peshmerga
fought for control of cities like Kirkuk, once it
became clear that we were on our own, there
was only one option. We ran.

For anywhere between one and a half to three
million Kurds, depending on which figures are
used, that meant heading for the mountains
and attempting to seek sanctuary in one of
Iraq's neighbouring countries. For my family
and me, that meant making the long journey
towards the Iraq-Iran border; the same journey
my uncle and his family had made so many
years earlier.

We travelled on foot, along with countless
other families from the camps. All the time,
we watched the skies. We had heard about the
no-fly zone, but it did not prohibit the use of
helicopters. I now know that we were right to
be afraid, because there are several stories of
helicopter gunships targeting refugee columns
along the way to the borders.

In the mountains, we kept going, with little in
the way of food or supplies. We had to melt snow
to get water as we climbed above the snow line.

Many people had no chance to prepare for the cold, but young or old, they had to keep going, hoping that they would get to safety before the army could catch up with them. We had no illusions about what would happen to us if we were caught this time. After all, what was there left for the regime to do to us except kill us? We had to get over the borders, so we walked.

Not that things were easy for those of my people who made it to the borders. There is footage of refugees at the border with Turkey, sitting on the mountainsides because there was nowhere else for them to go. Ahead of them stood a slender line of Turkish soldiers, ordered to hold them back and beating those who tried to cross, yet knowing that it would not work if all those there rushed them at once.

Iran was less hostile, but only marginally so. Its generals are rumoured to have encouraged the Iraqi regime to move quicker to deal with those of us trying to flee, and we quickly found ourselves stuck in refugee camps along the borders, with only tents to call home.

From escaping one camp, we had come to another, and we were no more free to leave than we had been there.

Worse, we were trapped tightly, not able to cross over into Iran, in exactly the right conditions for the Iraqi military to have killed us had it come quickly enough.

Then the rumours came. The military was coming. The helicopter gunships were coming. We found ourselves faced with what seemed like a choice between the guns of the Iranian border guards and those of the Iraqi military. Yet we knew that we had to take the chance of escaping.

Massoud Barzani commanded the peshmerga who held back the Iraqi military, while the rest of us crossed the border however we could. There are stories of people crossing through minefields, or ignoring soldiers who are preparing to shoot them on the way across. We made it through, heading into Iran. So many of the situations in my life have been tense, with the knowledge that I or my family could be hurt or killed. There was the moment in 1983 when I was thrown back as too small, the times the soldiers came to our house in the camp, all the times during the Anfal when we wondered if they were going to kill all of us in the camps. Yet this moment, running for our lives into a country that didn't want us, was probably the most terrifying of all. Maybe it was because, for this moment, I was finally old enough to understand just how dangerous the situation was.

There are so many ways it could have gone wrong. If the Iraqi military had been a little quicker, or if they had chosen to drop chemical weapons, we would have died. If the Iranian military had chosen not to let us through, or even if we had just been kept waiting there on the border until we starved... it was almost more likely in the aftermath of the failed revolt that we would die than that we would live.

Yet somehow, we made it through into Iran, deep enough that even the Iraqi military did not dare chase after us, for fear of sparking another war in the region. Yet that did not mean that we were free. The Iranian government was utterly unprepared for a humanitarian disaster on this scale, and probably did not want more refugees after the waves of my people forced to cross the borders in the past twenty five years.

The result was another camp, where we were forced to stay for months while the Iranian government tried to decide what to do with us. The facilities there were basic, because the camp had not been there for long, and because there were simply so many people fleeing Iraq. I think perhaps some of the Iranians were hoping that we would go back, but if so, they were mistaken.

Although it was hard going to Iran, in some ways, there were elements in place that made it easier. My family had relatives there, in the form of my uncle's family. There was already a solid PDK organisation in the country, able to negotiate with the Iranian government and slowly get people accepted into Iran. It is possible in some ways that we had more support waiting for us than those of my people who had to run in 1978. If so, then I can only imagine how hard things must have been for them.

While we escaped, peshmerga and those who could not run continued to fight for another six months. At the end of that time, the Iraqi army was forced to pull back, unable to definitively retake Dohuk, Erbil and Sulaymaniyah. So, how successful was the uprising? It failed to overthrow Saddam, or to finally create a free Kurdistan as a separate nation, but can it be called a failure on that basis? Perhaps outside commentators see it that way, and it is easy to see why, but the revolt should not be judged in relation to its unrealised potential, but instead in terms of what it did manage to do.

After all, it still achieved a great deal. With the no-fly zone in place from 1991, it was able to bring about at least the creation of a semi-autonomous Kurdish region, thanks to the peshmergas' success in pushing back the army. In that, it was able to lay the foundations for the Kurdistan that has arisen since 2003. It also helped to show us that Saddam could be beaten. The revolution the uprising promised might not have lasted for long, but while it did last, it showed just how vulnerable Saddam's position was. It also showed all of us the depth of the hatred so many people held for him.

More importantly, the uprising saved those of us who were trapped in the camps. I believe that it literally saved our lives, because it gave us a chance to get free before Saddam could finish what he started and kill us. After all, the response of his regime to every other time of crisis had been to attack my people in increasingly violent ways. What might he have done this time, when Kurdistan had openly risen up against him?

Instead of finding out, we were free. Not immediately, and not totally, because of the conditions in Iran, but we were free nonetheless. Thousands of people who had been taken in the Anfal, snatched from their own homes, or pushed into camps in 1978 had escaped. That might not have been the sole aim of the uprising, or even its main aim, but it was a success on a scale that dwarfed everything it achieved politically. It meant hardship on the long march to flee the country, but it also meant that people survived who might otherwise have died. It meant that finally, Saddam's programme of genocide had failed. For all the regime's power and planning, those of us it might have murdered in future were safe.

7

Rebuilding and civil war

How do you rebuild a nation when that nation is still not recognised as existing? How do individuals who have spent years trapped in camps rebuild their lives? What comes next after something on the scale of the genocide inflicted on my people?

The answer for that varied hugely for different people after 1991. For me, and for many of my people, the answer lay in moving around the world, building new lives in places where Saddam was only an occasional news story. There are hundreds of thousands of Kurds living away from the countries around Kurdistan, and many of them moved themselves or their families in the years after 1991. After just two years, I moved away from Kurdistan, having realised that after so long in an environment where I had no freedom to even go to the next town, I wanted to see more of the world.

I was able to travel, to build a life, a family and a business. Those are such simple things. Things which the majority of people probably don't think twice about. Yet had I remained in one of the camps, even if I had not been killed by now, none of those things would have been possible. I would not have been able to travel further than a razor wire topped fence. I would not have had the freedom to build up my own business, or to see it thrive. I would not have the family that I have, thousands of miles from Iraq.

I think perhaps that is one thing shared by the majority of people who got out of the camps alive. A sense of how precious even the most ordinary things are, so that they do not dare waste the life they have now. There is a kind of determination in those who were in the camps to be more than Saddam tried to reduce them to being. There are so many who have gone on to be doctors, lawyers, artists or more, because the thought of settling for an ordinary kind of life after the camps isn't one they couldn't allow. The years after 1991 were their chance and they knew that they had to take it.

For far too many of my people though, the years after 1991 meant lives filled with more violence, as civil war erupted throughout Kurdistan from 1994 on. As the army was forced to pull back, the PDK and PUK had primary control of separate areas of the north. Then, when they were able to conduct elections in 1992, they found that the new parliament of Kurdistan was split between them, not dominated by one or the other. While they were actively fighting against Saddam, they were able to work together, but once it seemed like that fight might be won, their differences gradually became too great for them to co-exist peacefully.

I am not going to try to inflame those differences here, but I would like to understand them. After all, we are all Kurds, and it seems wrong that we should have ended up fighting one another after decades of persecution by the regime. What could be so important that it drove families to split apart and cost thousands of lives? Partly, it comes down to long running questions over control of Kurdistan, and to differences that grew up in the years when neither party was able to act to free my people.

Yet we have still not answered the question of why that war started. Were long running differences enough? Alone, they probably would not have been, but in this case there were distinct economic stimuli to spark the conflict. In establishing their positions in the new Kurdistan, both sides wanted to dominate key economic resources, to ensure that they would be used for the good of the region. The oil resources of Kirkuk have been mentioned several times throughout this book as a source of conflict, and here again they had a role to play. Both sides felt that in order to be able to have a say in the future direction of Kurdistan, they needed to control that oil. In particular, they needed to control some of the black market trade in it with neighbouring countries.

All foreign trade was black market at that time, so there is certainly nothing wrong in either side having engaged in it. The UN had introduced trade embargoes on Iraq in an attempt to put pressure on Saddam's regime, but those embargoes applied to the whole country. Even to Kurdistan, a region that had effectively broken away from it, with its own anthem, flag and parliament. In addition to the UN sanctions, there was a blockade on trade to the rest of Iraq, imposed by the Bagdad government. That combination made control of black market trade routes crucial to ensuring that supplies got through for the areas of the country depending on each party.

In May 1994 the two sides were no longer in a position to solve things through negotiation. Fighting broke out between them. The usual reason given here is the ownership of a series of shops, but ultimately, I suspect that is designed to make everyone involved look petty. In fact, it seems more likely that they had just reached a point where the two parties needed to establish their relative strength, and I think in their eyes only violence would allow them to do it definitively. After so many years of fighting against the oppression of Saddam's regime, it probably seemed like the only solution available.

It was a solution that cost thousands of people their lives. Some commentators suggest that around 2,000 people were killed over just the next year, but figures for the whole conflict are scarce, taking in as they do what ended up as a three way conflict between the two main parties and the Iraqi army. It may be that we will never know how many people died in that conflict. I lost a brother to it, killed in fighting against the PKK.

Kurdistan as a whole almost lost far more than that. The civil war provided the Iraqi army with just the kind of opportunity it had been waiting for. When the two parties had been working together, they seemed too strong to take on. After months of conflict, weakened by fighting one another, they must have seemed like easy prey to the southern forces. In 1996 up to thirty thousand troops attacked Erbil and then Sulaymaniyah, withdrawing only after American cruise missile strikes warned them of the possibility of re-igniting the whole Iraq war.

This brings me to one of the most complex elements of the civil war, which is that in many ways it was not *just* a civil war. At different stages, it seems to have involved multiple incursions from outside Kurdistan, including ones from the Iraqi army, from Iran, from Turkey and from the US. These involvements from outside Kurdistan in many ways made the civil war a longer and more complex one than it needed to be, and also did a lot to change the way the conflict played out.

First, the involvement of the Iraqi army resulted in the driving out of the PUK from Erbil. When they left, that created a power vacuum in the city, and the PDK were able to secure the city. In Sulaymaniyah, the involvement of the Iranians seems to have brought about the opposite effect, creating a situation in which the PUK were able to take the city from the PDK.

In effect, what started as a civil war quickly became an extension of Iran and Iraq's on-going conflicts with one another. The Iraqi army seems to have come into the conflict at least partly in response to the involvement of the Iranians, and seems to have been to avoid the annexing of Kurdistan by Iran. Bagdad undoubtedly hated the idea of a free Kurdistan run by the two main parties, but Saddam's regime was probably arrogant enough to believe that eventually they would fail and it would regain the region. Iran invading, however, raised the possibility of that country controlling Kurdistan in the longer term and depriving Iraq of it. It was a possibility Iraq couldn't allow.

The involvement of the Americans was much less extensive. They attacked the advancing Iraqi forces in a limited fashion with missile strikes, though the effect of those strikes was enough to scare Bagdad into pulling back again. They acted to evacuate several thousand Kurds with pro-Western interests caught up in the fighting. Those including members of what was called the Iraqi National Congress, an organisation the US had backed, which was dedicated to the overthrow of Saddam Hussein. Members of it were executed along with peshmerga fighters after Erbil fell to the Iraqi army.

Then there was Turkey. Iran and Iraq might have become involved in the civil war anyway, because it represented an opportunity for both of them in Kurdistan, yet Turkey, which has hated my people for centuries, should never have played a part in the conflict. It did so primarily because it believed members of a third political party, the PKK or Kurdistan Workers' Party, were acting inside Kurdistan to attack anyone of Turkish descent they could find. The PKK had not been as active in Iraq as the PDK or PUK, but was a much larger party in Turkey, and was hated by its regime.

Turkish forces entered the country in 1997, and more than a thousand people died in the violence that followed, while and up to ten thousand more were displaced by it.

That involvement from Turkey both complicated the civil war and potentially gave it an excuse to interfere in Kurdistan again.

It wasn't until 1998 that the two sides were able to reach a permanent peace deal, brokered by the US, in the form of the Washington Agreement. There had been numerous cease-fires prior to that agreement, so it is hard to see why that one stuck when they did not. One possibility is that after four years of violence, both sides had finally decided that they'd had enough of it. Certainly, the human cost of the conflict was a high one, yet alone this doesn't seem like an adequate explanation.

Nor does the internationally brokered nature of the deal. Yes, it meant that the terms were being watched by someone outside Kurdistan, but that was true for several of the other cease-fires, and they did not hold. In any case, it is insulting to suggest that the only way peace in the region could be maintained was for America to step in and hold the sides apart politically, as though they were bickering children.

I suspect that a large part of the reason the Washington Agreement succeeded is that both the PUK and PDK had reached positions where they had a meaningful say over the future of Kurdistan, and which they could sustain. The PUK had Sulaymaniyah and most of Kirkuk, while the PDK had Erbil and Dohuk. They were sufficiently well balanced militarily that they could protect their areas from domination by the others, and also sufficiently well balanced that they were aware of the danger of the war continuing indefinitely.

I would like to think that played a large role in bringing about the peace. Although they have very different ideas about what is the best thing for Kurdistan, it must be acknowledged that *both* the PDK and PUK have generally acted in what they saw as the best interests of the country. By 1998, they must have seen that an on-going civil war costing thousands of lives and increasingly involving foreign military forces could never be in those interests. Peace was what my people needed.

So they signed the peace agreement. The peace has not always been an easy one, however. First, although Kurdistan is one region, it is essentially a region divided. To this day, there is a clear split between those areas that are PUK controlled and those that are PDK controlled. That is true to such an extent that after the signing of the agreement, people moved to live in the areas that matched their own political affiliations.

There is one party that I did not mention there, with good reason. The Washington Agreement stipulated many things about the division of the region between the parties, but it left no room for the PKK. Instead, it explicitly excluded the largely communist party from political life in Kurdistan, by saying that both the PDK and

PUK would work against them. That condition was a necessary one to prevent further action by Turkey, but may also have suited American sensibilities too by excluding the possibility of communist politicians in the region. Whatever the reason, it is an exclusion that has added to tensions in the long run by driving the PKK underground, but may have made the peace more workable in the short term by keeping it as a bilateral agreement between the parties with real power.

How do we count the cost of the civil war? I have already said above that in terms of a simple body count, it is almost impossible to quantify. Yet we can see a number of effects of the civil war that need to be addressed. There is the simplest effect; that it killed people and caused damage to property. It meant that there was more to rebuild once the region's key parties were in a position to begin doing so and that during the civil war, there was more pain and misery for those caught up in it.

There is the delay in rebuilding that it caused. My people could have had twenty plus years in which to rebuild Kurdistan. Instead, they have had a little over a decade.

They have done a marvellous job in that time, putting in infrastructure, building hospitals, schools and transport hubs such as airports, but how much more could they have achieved if they had not been at war until 1998?

There is the lack of trust that the civil war caused. Even today, Kurdistan can feel almost more like several separate regions held together by a joint political will than like one place. Although it is fading, the things that happened during the civil war turned my people against one another, and there is a lingering feeling that something like that could so easily happen again. It is one reason why I have tried to be careful to avoid apportioning blame in this chapter so far. Kurdistan does not need more blame. It needs its major political parties to work together in the interests of the region.

The issue of blame can be a difficult one. Civil wars can be vicious, and with the one in Kurdistan, there are, almost inevitably, accusations that both sides resorted to the sort of tactics that might have been better left to Saddam's regime. People went missing, and have not been seen since. People were almost certainly murdered.

Compensation has been offered to the families of those involved, but governments can rarely decide that things are ended so neatly, and the accusations continue to make political life difficult in Kurdistan.

I am not bringing up those issues to attack anyone politically. Nor do I intend to focus on specific instances that might be seen as apportioning fault. This is not about that. It is about the way the past needs to be acknowledged in order to move on from it. I do not feel that it is in any way against Kurdistan to talk about some of the things that happened in the civil war, as some people seem to feel. There are people who react angrily to any mention that such things might have been done, and that the best option on damaging issues like this is to pretend that they do not exist, so that the world sees that Kurdistan is great. Yet I would argue the opposite. Kurdistan *is* great, and it is *because* it is great that it needs to question things when they are wrong. As a people, we are at a unique point in our history. We have the capacity to make Kurdistan almost anything we want it to be. It cannot be a place where people can disappear and it goes unchallenged, or we have made it the same place that Saddam's Iraq was.

The political consequences of the civil war spread beyond the domestic sphere though. When the Coalition forces invaded Iraq in 2003, Kurdistan was the only part of the country that was stable, but there was still no talk of making it fully independent. Nor have there been major efforts from outside Kurdistan to that end since. There are many reasons for that, ranging from the need for stability in Iraq as a whole to the attitudes of surrounding countries, but at least one contributing element must have been fear.

Fear that, for all that it is stable now, Kurdistan might still pull itself apart on political lines in the future. It seems likely that the civil war has cost Kurdistan a lot on the path to independence, including the level of international respect it should have.

Yet despite all the difficulties created for Kurdistan both by Saddam's regime and the civil war, it has rebuilt itself. The Kurdistan Regional Government has worked hard in that. Here, I would like to outline a few of the more important achievements, but remember that they are only parts of a greater picture. The rebuilding of Kurdistan isn't just the largest projects. It is every house rebuilt that had been destroyed in the village clearances of the Anfal. It is the creation of infrastructure to connect to a world that had trade embargoes against the region just a few years ago. It is even social change, such as the women who are able to go to our universities or join our police force where just a few years ago, we had to deny them to live to the standards imposed on us by others. Some of these aspects have been briefly discussed elsewhere, but they deserve to be looked at again here.

Let's take Kurdistan's first international airport, in Erbil. It stands on the site of a former military airbase, closed in 1991 by a combination of the rebellion and the no-fly zone.

The continuation of the no-fly zone and the isolation of Kurdistan from the rest of Iraq meant that it was only at the start of 2003, with the fall of Saddam, that the KRG could consider building a regional airport. It quickly became a symbol of the rest of the rebuilding effort, and it was a point of pride that the first planes were landing there before the end of the year.

Or consider the case of the University of Dohuk[15], which uses a variety of buildings seized during the uprising, from a Ba'ath party headquarters to the former prison, and which sprang up over the course of mere months. People there started it with no funding, few facilities, and little equipment or books, making the most of volunteers to teach the courses in the early days.

In cases like this, the same pattern repeated itself again and again. Whatever was left behind when the Bagdad regime's forces were driven out was reused, often in unexpected ways.

Difficulties were overcome mostly through the willingness of the people involved to do whatever was necessary to make things work, but also because often, those involved didn't know that things should be any different.

When you have never been allowed a university, why should one that isn't adequately funded be a problem?

There have been massive leaps forward made in terms of urban renewal and the building of new homes since 2003. Part of that is replacing the buildings damaged either under the regime or during the civil war. Another part of it has been building on any available spaces to find homes for the people displaced by the conflicts, for the ones returning to Kurdistan from Iran or elsewhere, and simply for those coming to Kurdistan in search of a better life in the most stable part of the country.

One result of this is that many of the old camps used to imprison us have been entirely redeveloped. In several cases, if I did not know that they were there, it would be hard to recognize them as what they were. It may seem odd that people want to live in them now, when so many people suffered in those same places, yet that is one of the things about the tide of change in Kurdistan: it tends to wash away whatever was there before.

Another area of rebuilding has been with Kurdistan's villages. This has, in many ways, been a more difficult project for the KRG and its allies than some others. There has been a drive to rebuild as many of the four thousand or so villages destroyed under Saddam as possible, and there has been a lot of international aid money for that project, but despite that, Kurdistan remains largely urban.

It seems that this is one area where it is not simply a case of rebuilding, but one where it is necessary to persuade people that they might want a rural life, rather than all the advantages brought by living in a city.

That is one of the things that Kurdistan is slowly addressing, and there are others. The initial phase of the rebuilding was largely a physical one. It was a case of putting together bricks and mortar, which we could always do, and buying in what we could not get ourselves using money from Kurdistan's oil reserves. Yet the rebuilding of Kurdistan is also a social project. It is about building a nation as well as building houses.

With that, some aspects have gone very well. Kurdistan has an elected government that is responsive to its people and that is actively trying to make a better region. It has a sense of identity in symbols such as its flag and anthem, as well as a place in the world that it is cementing through having its own ambassadors. Some social issues, such as the place of women in Kurdistan, have been addressed more slowly. Yet the key thing is that there *is* a commitment to handling serious social issues and building the kind of society that the people of Kurdistan deserve.

And it is working, piece by piece. Women have a bigger place in Kurdistan than in any of the surrounding countries. They can be found in Kurdistan's armed forces and police, among its politicians and business leaders. The booming Kurdish economy and rebuilding processes in particular have provided many women with opportunities to make their names as investors, alongside their male counterparts.

Why is the shape of the rebuilding in Kurdistan as it is? Why has the physical rebuilding been so amazingly fast? Why has the non-physical side of things taken more time? Why does it seem that politically, Kurdistan has moved fastest with its international relations, when the priority for most new governments is usually internal politics?

There are several factors at play here. One is where Kurdistan has come from. In previous chapters, we have talked about mass exoduses involving millions of Kurdistan's inhabitants, the destruction of almost every village there, and the deaths of tens of thousands of people. With such a blank canvas, the physical elements were the immediate priority. Physical changes were also more immediately noticeable because of that almost 'blank canvass' starting point. A village among thousands more would not be noticeable, but one constructed where there were almost none before definitely is.

The resources available to the KRG may have affected the shape and speed of rebuilding too.

We have seen above that the government took control of many buildings formerly used by the Ba'ath party or the Iraqi military. That gave them a stock of locations to use for a number of major projects, such as Erbil's airport. It gave them buildings in what were often key locations, with the best access to infrastructure of any buildings around their cities. In most cities around the world, there is not that stock of unused buildings in key sites. Instead, there is a constant fight to try to find locations that will work, often accompanied by the need to build from scratch. The availability of captured buildings meant that for many large scale projects, the KRG had a head start.

Monetarily, too, the KRG had good resources available to it. There was the money from Kirkuk's oil fields, giving it a strong source of income, but there was also the fact of Kurdistan's relatively small population in relation to its size, particularly in the first years of the rebuilding. That smaller population meant that it could be self-sufficient in terms of food, allowing money to be spent on other things such as the rebuilding of the country.

Additionally, there was international aid. Although the international community has been slow to assist Kurdistan militarily, it has poured aid money into it. That money came into Kurdistan through a combination of the obvious need of the region's situation, through its stability in relation to the rest of Iraq, and, perhaps more cynically, through the ease with which aid agencies could demonstrate that they were doing something. They could see villages and towns being rebuilt, and they could say to their superiors that they were achieving something.

Perhaps that international aid is one reason why Kurdistan's politics have had something of an international focus. By carving a place for itself in the international agenda separately from Iraq; by having its own ambassadors and anthem, its own international visits and identity, Kurdistan was able to attract some of the help it needed in rebuilding itself directly, rather than having to wait for funds to be funnelled through the rest of Iraq, possibly never to arrive. Kurdistan needed to ensure that it was not forgotten in the rebuilding the way it was forgotten while it was being destroyed.

Yet obviously, Kurdistan's promotion of itself on the international stage is down to far more than that. Pride, for example. It is one thing that practically all the Kurds I meet in Kurdistan share: a sense of pride in Kurdistan as a region and as a potential nation. That pride played a huge role in the rebuilding process. It meant that people weren't prepared to settle for just creating the bare minimum the region needed to survive, when they could strive to make it great. It is that pride that led to the people of Dohuk working together to produce their university (and now starting work on an airport), or to the KRG pushing on with rebuilding projects at such a blistering pace that towns could become unrecognisable in the course of a few months. It is that pride that led to the installation of world class telecommunications infrastructure, while the rest of Iraq lagged behind.

When the people of Kurdistan talk about it being a second Dubai, it is not just a dream, it is a statement of intent. People in Kurdistan have so much pride in the region, and in many ways, the politicians have to work hard to keep up with the level of ambition the people have for it. They feel that they have to keep making demonstrable improvements just to keep Kurdistan's people happy. Perhaps that is part of the reason why so much of the early rebuilding was focussed on big, visible but quickly completed projects like the airport, rather than on the sort of deep social and political reconstruction that is often slow, tricky and hard to pin down.

One final factor in the reconstruction, and the reason why I have included both in the same chapter, is the civil war. For me, it is the most important aspect in explaining both the speed and shape of Kurdistan's reconstruction. For speed, there is the fact that the politicians had seen how bad things could get. They had seen how quickly political violence could come if they did not find ways to show that they belonged at the top, and so they had to find ways to show the populace that they were improving their lives. Slowing down was not an option.

That is particularly the case when the two main parties were locked almost in the reconstruction equivalent of an arms race. Operating out of largely separate areas, each one was in a position to receive direct credit for any projects completed in their areas, and so seem to have set out to outdo one another. When one completed a housing project, the other had to produce one.

When Erbil acquired its airport, Sulaymaniyah had to start work on one too. The competition between the PDK and PUK has manifested itself in a continuous desire to gain support through the rebuilding process.

It may seem like a strange kind of competition to have grown up, but it is considerably better for the people of Kurdistan than fighting, and should be welcomed.

The influence of the civil war has also changed the shape of the recovery. The competition and the desire to be seen to be doing as much as possible have combined to produce an emphasis on the most visible projects, while the desire to avoid conflict has perhaps meant the putting off of some of the most difficult political questions.

Nevertheless, the speed of Kurdistan's recovery has been stunning. Since 1998, it has undergone a transformation that most countries could only dream of. Let alone a country that had spent as much time as Kurdistan being repressed previously. For so many other countries, the end of repression has meant a slow grind to recovery. For Kurdistan, it meant a rapid flowering that goes on to this day.

It is crucial that it continues.. The regime did so much to hurt my people, yet every step that Kurdistan takes forward is another one it takes away from that past. Every new school, every new home, is a sign that Saddam's regime did not destroy my people. Instead, they are now in a better position within Iraq than they have ever been, moving closer and closer to the point where it could finally be what we have hoped for over so long... a country of our own.

8

Genocide – a lesson we do not learn from

Genocide is an attempt to destroy or partially destroy a racial, ethnic, religious or other group. It is a crime that simultaneously seems impossible to understand, yet in some ways has its roots in impulses that are all too easy to both comprehend and give in to. It seems impossible to understand because of its sheer scale. Most of us, thankfully, would not pretend to understand how one human being can murder another. We like to feel that we would never do it, almost regardless of the circumstances. So how can we hope to understand murder that runs to thousands, tens of thousands, or hundreds of thousands of people? How can we hope to try to understand the systematic destruction of a people, not just through their murder, but also through the replacement of their culture, their displacement from their homes, and a level of day to day oppression that no one should have to live with?

Yet at the same time, we all carry the impulses that seed such actions within us. As humans, we seem to notice differences at least as much as similarities, and to react to those differences whenever we see them in people. The same instinct that makes me take pride in being Kurdish also has a darker half that needs to be controlled, if it is not to become contempt for anything that is not like us.

It is an instinct that has won out again and again through history, and that is something I want to explore here. In this chapter, I want to look beyond Kurdistan to genocides that have occurred around the world in modern history, briefly exploring the ways each came into being, its similarities to what happened to my people, and the ways in which the world responded.

I want to do this for a couple of reasons. Firstly, I want to leave you with no doubt in your mind that what happened in Kurdistan was an extended programme of genocide, following a classic pattern. Secondly, I want to look at the issues raised by all of these genocides, including that of my people, and ask what we can learn from them. Will we ever be in a world free of them? What can the international community can do when they occur, or are they condemned to watching from the side lines while people die?

I do not intend to go into great depth with any one of these genocides. I do not pretend to be an expert on them, or on the subject generally.

As such, it is possible that I will get details wrong here, or miss out on some of the context. Nevertheless, I think it is important to at least begin to explore other instances of genocide if we are to see the suffering of my people in its proper context.

There is no easy place to start with a subject like this, but let's begin with probably the largest genocide of the modern era, the holocaust of the Jews in Nazi Germany. How, in the course of just a few years, did a modern, industrialised nation set about murdering probably more than 6 million people from one religious/ethnic group?

It seems to have happened incrementally though with a familiarly fixed objective in mind. From 1933 onwards, Hitler's Nazi party took progressive steps towards the repression of the Jewish community, limiting their involvement in public life and subjecting them to arbitrary detention. From 1938, following Germany's union with Austria, they were placed in concentration camps. At that point, a committee was due to be formed to help those Jews fleeing Hitler, but no country wanted to help them. Germany forcibly expelled more than 17,000 Polish Jews in the same year, but Poland would not accept them.

From September 1939, following the outbreak of war, Jews began to be rounded up in greater numbers, often into ghettos of larger cities, with the intention of making the eventual 'final solution' easier. Forced labour was instituted for many. In 1940, the programme moved on to mass murder, with individual pogroms in occupied areas killing Jews in their thousands as troops swept through them, sending those they did not kill to a new generation of concentration camps. From 1941, this 'final solution' expanded dramatically, with the SS sweeping all occupied lands, killing or capturing all Jews they could find. It is probably at this stage that concentration camps such as Auschwitz started experimenting with Zyklon-B gas, though the gas chambers there did not come into use as a tool of industrial mass murder for another year.

As the war ended in 1945, there were attempts to destroy the evidence. Crematoria were ordered demolished, and many concentration camp victims were marched hundreds of miles from their places of imprisonment. Documents were destroyed, but enough were recovered to give a picture of what was occurring when coupled with testimony from those involved. Yet even today, there are those who deny it happened, thanks to those destructions of evidence, and those who do not want it to be true for political reasons.

From there, let's turn to a much more recent

example, in the form of the 'ethnic cleansing' that took place in the former Yugoslavia from 1993. The disintegration of the Balkan states is complex, but involved the growth of nationalism in numerous smaller areas that are now states, such as Serbia, Croatia and Macedonia. Leaders such as Slobodan Milosevic were determined to craft the largest and most prosperous regions for 'their' people, and Milosevic in particular seems to have been determined to treat the whole of the former Yugoslavia as a kind of larger Serbia.

Bosnia was caught in the middle, with a large Serbian population claiming much of its territory as part of Serbia or exclusively Serbian republics. The violence this sparked drove out many of Bosnia's Croats and Bozniaks, forcing them into smaller and smaller areas of the country while the UN refused to intervene. When it finally did, protecting a few small 'safe areas', mainly protecting Bosnia's Muslim population, those proved to be anything but safe. Instead, UN peacekeepers were forced to stand by while Serbian forces took control of all but the one around Sarajevo and killed those within. In 1995 Serbian troops followed that up by attacking the largely Muslim town of Srebrenicia, shelling it until up to 6,000 people tried to take refuge in a Dutch staffed UN compound, while 20,000 more could not gain entrance.

Those same Serbian troops, under Ratco Mladic, camp to the camp with trucks, separating the men and boys from the women and children outside the camp and taking them away while the UN troops did nothing (although they *could* do nothing, given their small numbers). The next day, they took the women outside the camp. Over the next two, they came for those within it. Perhaps 7,500 men and boys were killed and left in mass graves. The term 'ethnic cleansing' was used for this, specifically to avoid the use of the term 'genocide'.

Another example can be seen in Rwanda in 1994-1995. This genocide had been a long time in the making, coming out of tensions between Hutu and Tutsi inhabitants of the country. The Tutsis, originally herders and tribesmen, had been placed over the Hutus by the Belgians in colonial times, but had been displaced by civil war from the 1950s. They had been progressively stripped of rights after that, with restrictions placed on them teaching or attending university. They continued resistance against the Hutus; a conflict that helped to keep old hatreds alive.

Those hatreds broke into full civil war in 1990, with a ceasefire following in 1993. However, in 1994, following the death of President Habyarimana in a plane crash brought about by an extremist, Hutus blamed Tutsis for his death, or at least saw it as the excuse they needed. The next hundred days saw Hutu mobs slaughtering any Tutsis they could find, along with any Hutus thought to be too 'moderate', primarily for believing that Tutsis should not be murdered, or for having Tutsi friends and relations. It created a situation where the only way to avoid being killed was to join in with the violence, with the result that anywhere from half a million to a million people may have died. Most commentators put the final death toll at around 800,000, but there was much additional violence, including the systematic use of rape and infection with HIV/AIDs against the female Tutsi population.

There were UN peacekeeping forces in the country at the time, but the UN commander on the ground got only around half the troops he asked for, and even that number was designed for a routine peacekeeping operation, rather than for the prevention of a country-wide genocide. In any case, the forces were well aware that they had no mandate to intervene, and so frequently had to stand by while massacres occurred. The UN resisted calls to label the events on the ground as a genocide at the time, and was reluctant to intervene.

The genocide did not leave the paper trail that other genocides had before, but it was still highly organised. Rwanda's government, under

Prime Minister Jean Kambanda, did much to support the genocide, helping to form militias consisting mainly of younger men who did the majority of the killing. Those militias were supplied with vehicles, weapons and fuel to allow them to reach every part of the country. The army even supported them where they met resistance.

There was also a strong propaganda element to the genocide, with radio and TV transmissions stressing hatred of the Tutsis, helping to fuel an atmosphere in which genocide could take place. Radio Rwanda in particular broadcast warnings that Tutsis were planning to murder Hutus, prompting Hutus to attack Tutsis first. Other radio stations emphasised the idea that Tutsi fighters from their resistance movement would be mingling with the civilian population, looking just like everybody else.

As in so many genocides, there was an emphasis on targeting higher concentrations of Tutsis, driven to supposedly 'safe' areas like schools, hospitals, or aid compounds. There is evidence of Tutsis being rounded up and killed by friends and people they knew, either caught up in the propaganda of hatred or simply afraid of being added to the list of sympathisers. Following the genocide, millions of Hutus fled the country, fearful of reprisals, and ended up in aid camps in Zaire and the Congo, staying there while the Tutsis took power in Rwanda. They were forced back from 1996, but there were relatively few arrests or trials for the genocide in the aftermath.

Finally, although there are many, many more genocides we could consider, I want to look at one of the world's most recent genocides, in Sudan. As a country, it has many similarities with Iraq, from being ruled by an ex-general (Omar Bashir) since 1989, to a simmering tension between two broad ethnic groups, in the form of African farmers and largely Arab tribes moving through the area.

There had been tensions ever since Bashir's rise to the presidency, on ethnic as well as religious lines, but those only turned into open conflict from 2003 in the Darfur region. At that point, the organisations the Sudan Liberation Army and the Justice and Equality Movement took up arms complaining about attacks by nomads in the region, as well as a lack of attention from the government.

The response from the government was to unleash mounted Arab Janjaweed militias, allowing them to attack villages within the Darfur region at will, using murder, rape, theft and mutilation as weapons of terror against the non-Arab population. African farmers were systematically removed from their lands, and whole villages destroyed. More than 400,000 people died, while around 1.5millon more were displaced, forced to seek refuge in neighbouring countries. The current solution to the crisis has involved the recognition of South Sudan as a separate country, although tensions remain high in the north.

There are many more genocides than this. I have not gone into details about the genocide in Cambodia in 1975 or that in Guatemala in 1982. I have not explored earlier genocides either, or events which are not generally labelled as such, but which seem to meet the basic criteria of one. There simply is not sufficient space to discuss them all here, which I think says something very unpleasant about humanity and its capacity for violence. I will try to mention them where appropriate below.

Those I have included share a number of points, both with one another and with what happened to my people. Not every circumstance is identical, and I will try to explore some of the differences as well as the similarities, but there are several key points that emerge very clearly when looking at the situations above.

One is that these situations do not seem to have come out of nowhere. Genocide is not a single event, but is rather the endpoint of a process, involving the building of hatred and tensions. With Germany, we saw that the death camps were simply the end point of an on-going process of repression aimed at the Jews. The same was true in Rwanda, where we have already seen that Tutsis were excluded from many areas of public life.

In Kurdistan, the early cultural repression was less obvious. Indeed, in some respects such as our ability to express our culture, we were freer in Iraq than in many of the surrounding countries. Yet there was a definite progression in hatred on the part of the regime, from early measures such as small scale village clearances and camp construction in the 1970s, through on-going persecution, to the beginnings of mass murder for limited groups of us and finally a large scale programme of extermination during the Anfal. There also was a measure of cultural obliteration in the teaching of our children in Arabic and the emphasis on propaganda aimed at making us love Saddam.

The way people still say "Saddam" points to another common factor in several of these events, which was the presence of a charismatic leader. Whether it was Hitler or Pol Pot, Slobodan Milosevic in Bosnia or Charles Taylor in Sierra Leone, the worst crimes against humanity seem so often to happen at the behest of a leader able to convince others that evil things are the right ones to do. I argue elsewhere that there is a danger in looking at things this way, because it means we look at a single individual rather than the actions of the many involved, but certainly, those charismatic leaders seem to play a part. Perhaps it is because, in any situation like this, even when there is a group willingness to repress a particular group, it takes someone to insist on the next steps. In Iraq, we have a clear example of this role of the leader in Saddam's insistence on the repeating of the fifth Anfal when it was not thorough enough for his tastes. In other situations, it has been far harder to prove that kind of direct link, even when it seems clear that there must have been one, as with the lack of signed orders from Hitler for the final solution, even though it seems clear that he approved it.

Yet behind that kind of charismatic leader, there was also, in each case, a political machine committed to the same ends. Indeed, in several cases, it is easy to see that the genocides were only able to take place as they did once less extreme figures from the countries' governments were out of the way. Take Rwanda again, where President Habyarimana's death not only provided the excuse for the genocide, but also removed a figure more interested in national unity than Jean Kambanda. Or take the troubles in Bosnia, which only began to surface in the wake of the death of General Tito, who served as a unifying figure. Even in Iraq, we can see that the worst atrocities against my people only began as Saddam Hussein gained more power from President al-Bakr, with our forced movement into camps only coming in 1978, after he had gained effective control in 1976, and the worst atrocities coming in the 1980s, once he was president. With Hitler's Germany, we can see that process over the course of more than a decade, with the gradual consolidation of power by the Nazi party coming alongside greater repression for the Jews.

That level of control was necessary in each case, because all of the genocides above had, not just official sanction, but active support from the governments or militaries involved in the areas. In the Balkans, for example, the atrocities were carried out by the official armed forces of the warring factions. In Sudan, the Janjaweed were government backed and supplied. In Rwanda, the killing might have been done by loosely organised militias, but those were supplied by the government, and supported by the military where necessary. In Nazi Germany, the whole organization of the genocide was done on an industrial scale. In Iraq, the same thing is clearly visible. The genocide was carried out by the government, using the military. It was occasionally blamed on other factions, but it was never done through intermediaries.

Unless we count the Jash, those Kurds pressed into service in the Iraqi army. They were often employed in the follow up to attacks during the

Anfal, because my people would be more likely
to surrender to them than to non-Kurds. Is there
a parallel for that? There is at least one obvious
one, though it is not exact, in the use of Jews
as helpers in the concentration camps, forcing
them to take part in the process of exterminat-
ing their own people. There is also something
of the same feeling in the way people in the
Rwandan genocide found themselves pushed
into killing friends and neighbours for fear of
being labelled as moderates and killed in turn.

What about the tactics employed? This is
where the greatest range of variations occurs,
since tactics tend to be dictated by individual
situations and the availability of weapons.
Rwanda's murder with machetes is not the
same as Bosnia's careful trucking out to places
of execution by firing squad or Nazi Germany's
use of gas chambers. Yet such a wide range of
different tactics of destruction were used across
Kurdistan that if we look closer, it is easy to
see that there are similarities with all of these
genocides.

If we take the early village clearances, for
example, there is a clear parallel to be found
in Sudan. There, Arab nomads were employed
to clear villages of indigenous African farmers,
forcing three times as many people to seek
refuge in nearby countries as they killed. They
took what they could, destroyed what they

could not, and killed anyone who tried to stop them. Or look at the Khmer Rouge's efforts in Cambodia. There, in an almost exact reversal of events in Kurdistan, they forced the urban populations to live in rural communes, killing thousands as part of the process.

I suspect the idea of rounding people up in camps will be familiar to those who have studied any of the genocides above, too. It happened on its largest scale in Nazi Germany, but also has parallels elsewhere, though not always in the way people might think. Refugee camps and supposed 'safe zones' could do the same job of clustering large numbers of a hated people together just as efficiently as establishing concentration camps. I am not saying that those running them were doing anything other than genuinely trying to help in each situation, on the contrary, I welcome their efforts to assist people when most others did not. I *am* saying that the overall effect of things like the Bosnian safe zones was similar in practice to that of the camps established for my people by Saddam's regime. They kept people in a defined area where it turned out that they could do nothing to defend themselves when their would-be murderers came for them. If there were not the same kind of camps in Bosnia, it was only because the advancing Serbian military did not need them.

There is a chilling similarity between the tactics employed in Srebrenica and those used against Barzani men and boys ten years before. There is the same sense of the military coming in and people being powerless to do anything but cooperate, the same systematic taking of people from within a closed environment, and the same sorting out of men and boys "of fighting age" from the rest. The fates of those taken seem to have been identical as well, right down to the identification of mass graves.

Both Sudan and Nazi Germany show us the tactics of sweeping an area. In Nazi held Europe, where troops scoured occupied towns and villages, killing any Jews they could find or deporting them to concentration camps. The same tactics employed in much of the Anfal, and not dissimilar to the Janjaweed raids on Sudanese villages in Darfur.

Then there is the use of chemical weapons. The Nazi use of Zyklon-B gas, along with other lethal cocktails of chemicals, is probably the best parallel here. The method of delivery was different, confined to specific gas chambers or to vans brought along when sweeping occupied lands, but the similarity is clear. The use of more indiscriminate methods by the Iraqi military is probably down to the existence of a well-defined Kurdish area in Kurdistan.

Then there are the propaganda campaigns to

consider. Many of these brutal atrocities have been accompanied by systematic propaganda campaigns aimed at doing several things simultaneously. They usually sought to minimise or distort perceptions of what was going on, as with the Bosnian insistence on the term 'ethnic cleansing' in preference to 'genocide'. They sought to reinforce people's commitment to the violence, as with the exhortations of Rwanda's radio stations. They also sought to reinforce the authority of the regime doing the killing, as in Nazi Germany.

These elements were present in Kurdistan. The most obvious was the general wave of propaganda supporting Saddam, whether it was the support for him on Iraqi TV or simply making us sing songs praising him as children. There was also an attempt to confuse us over Halabja by blaming the Iranians. As for evidence of propaganda supporting the genocide, there are the regime's repeated references to all Kurds as 'traitors' to consider. That seems part of the same kind of process of dehumanisation that had the Rwandan regime describing Tutsis as cockroaches.

Let's look at a difference now, when it comes to the question of scale. Obviously, the genocides outlined above involved vastly different numbers of dead and displaced people. The Holocaust involved more dead than all of the others I have cited put together. Yet does that make any one of them less of a genocide? I would argue that it does not. The intention was there in each case to attack or wipe out a people.

Indeed, the range of casualty figures here in some ways makes it more obvious that what happened in Kurdistan was genocide. They show that an event does not have to live up to the monstrous numbers of dead produced by the holocaust to qualify as this most evil of crimes. Bosnia in particular seems to have produced slightly lower numbers of dead in some of its worst atrocities, yet I cannot imagine those reading it would see what happened in Srebrenica or the safe zones as anything less than an attempt at genocide.

Except of course that people have. Famously, the term 'ethnic cleansing' was adopted around the world specifically to avoid using that term. It is one final similarity between all of these genocides, which is that, at the time or soon after, there were attempts made to hide what happened and even to deny that it had happened at all.

So we have the Holocaust deniers, who persist in claiming that because pieces of evidence destroyed by the Nazis are not there, we can never prove that the holocaust happened. They keep doing so even to the extent where several countries have had to make it a crime, just to keep the truth alive. We have repeated references to 'atrocities' in Sudan, without them being recognized as a genocide. Serbia is reduced to 'ethnic cleansing' rather than the real crime committed there. Even in Rwanda, which seemed to be so open about its crimes at the time, the Hutus who fled once the Tutsis came back to power were quick to clarify that they had been involved in mass murder rather than genocide.

Again and again, we can find attempts to hide what was done, whether in the destruction of documents or in the re-burying of the dead, as seems to have happened in Serbia. These are crimes that so often seem to take place openly, yet simultaneously manage to be quite hidden. The allies knew of Germany's hatred of the Jews, for example, but seem to have affected surprise at the existence of the concentration camps.

And always, always, there is that need to say that an event does not qualify as genocide. Why is that? Why avoid that word? There are complex reasons for the non-involvement of other countries in Iraq, which I will go into in the next chapter, but there is one key issue here, which is that genocide is one of the few things in international law that allows, even *requires*, international intervention. Ordinarily, countries are explicitly forbidden from interfering militarily in one another's sovereign territories, or from trying to control their internal affairs. Genocide, however, is supposed to warrant more than that. It is a rule that is supposedly designed to make it easier to avoid a repeat of the horrors of World War Two, yet in practice, it has allowed genocide to flower.

Why? Because of the apparent obligation the term creates. Mere mass murder is an internal matter. Brutal anti-insurrection campaigns and reigns of terror are internal matters. Slaughtering the inhabitants of a city, using chemical weapons against civilians, filling mass graves with truck-loads of men and boys… they are all apparently none of the rest of the world's business. Yet use the word genocide, and a country is saying that it is prepared to intervene. To commit its resources and lives, regardless of the political situation. Worse, if a country is found guilty of genocide, then merely having allies in the UN won't stop a military intervention. Just the word is enough.

Which is why everyone seems to be so determined to avoid the term. It creates an obligation at the time, and afterwards, it creates political embarrassment. Go back and call something a genocide, and the international community is saying that it should have intervened. Call the mass murder of Bosnians by their Serb neighbours anything but 'ethnic cleansing' and the

UN is saying that its troops should not have stood by to allow it. Recognize it in the Sudan, and suddenly, more than a peacekeeping force is involved. It has become the word no one dare say for fear of the consequences.

Yet perhaps there are other reasons why it is not officially applied to Kurdistan at the time. Perhaps there are legitimate arguments against it. In the interests of balance, I will consider some of those possible arguments here, along with their strengths and weaknesses.

It might be possible to argue, for example, that Saddam's troops were targeting an area rather than a specific ethnic group. After all, they destroyed whole villages, without specifically targeting the Kurds within. Yet that approach does not work. Kurdistan's rural areas were so overwhelmingly Kurdish that the argument is moot, while the process of Arabization in urban areas suggests a definite racial element to the violence.

Our imaginary critic could suggest that the tactic of imprisonment did not amount to the destruction of the Kurds, and that in any case, Saddam's campaigns mirrored earlier tactics employed in the region. I would argue in response that the imprisonment seems likely to have been a preliminary step to more murder, that tactics such as the bombing of villages with chemical weapons were new, and that the continuity in fact points to exactly the kind of continuous hatred of my people that we would expect before a genocide according to the examples above. In any case, for all the imprisonments and displacements, 182,000 people were killed.

The same counter argument applies to another issue, which is over whether the cultural destruction of a people counts in this context. Genocide is generally framed in such a way as to only include the physical destruction of a people, so attempts to destroy their cultures and traditions, for example by refusing to allow them to learn in their language or by cutting them off from their rural homes, seem to be a part of something else. Yet I would argue that this element does a lot to help to prove the genocidal intent of Saddam's forces. They were not just trying to kill people in an area, but specifically to destroy the Kurds, and key traces of Kurdishness along the way. Saddam occasionally wearing Kurdish clothing does not change that. It simply shows the way the regime sought to control and twist Kurdish cultural elements, mixing them up with something Arab until there was nothing of the original left.

Another argument might be that what Saddam's forces did was just a brutal counter insurgency campaign, full of individual crimes against the civilian population, but not amounting to genocide. It is an argument that is actually spurred by Saddam's brutality, on the basis that his troops killed plenty of people who were not Kurds as well as plenty who were. The deciding factor, this argument says, was whether people stood up to him, not their ethnicity.

This seems to be the approach taken by many official sources, and it is in some ways the strongest. What I would like to point out, however, is that many of the genocides outlined above took place in circumstances involving uprising, civil wars or other conflicts. Indeed, a high pressure, violent trigger is sometimes seen as one of the necessary components of a genocide, alongside a highly organised state, repression of a particular group and a charismatic leader.

Just because a genocide happens in the context of multiple on-going uprisings, that does not make it any less of a genocide. Instead, those circumstances are actually the most likely ones in which a government will move from specific counter-insurgency tactics to targeting a whole people on the basis that they are somehow all to blame for the rebellion of some of their members. That is very definitely what happened in Iraq, with Saddam describing all Kurds as 'traitors'. Counter-insurgency may have been the start, but his actions ceased to be aimed at peshmerga a long time before the Anfal.

The long refusal by many governments to acknowledge what happened in Kurdistan as a genocide may even have contributed to those genocides that came after the Anfal. I can all too readily imagine Milosevic, the Rwandans, and those like them laughing about how Saddam got away with genocide, and so they could too. Why not, in a world that refuses to acknowledge its existence?

Of course, the definition of genocide will continue to be reshaped as countries squirm to avoid defining anything as one. Yet a definition of genocide that somehow fails to include Kurdistan, Bosnia or some of the other places I have outlined in this chapter is simply too narrow to be realistic. We need a broader definition and the will to intervene if we are to stop such a thing from happening again and again.

Yet does that will exist? Will it ever? To understand that, we need to understand the full range of international responses to what happened in Kurdistan, and the full extent to which other countries were complicit in this genocide.

9

Acknowledging history for a better future

Why? As human beings faced with terrible events, it is one question that we almost inevitably ask. Why did it happen? Was there anything that could have been done to stop it? Crucially, could it happen again? Those are the questions I would like to ask here. Because I firmly believe that we, and the international community, have not learned enough lessons from what happened to prevent the atrocities perpetrated against my people from happening elsewhere in the world.

Let's start with the question of why Saddam's genocide against my people happened. There is a temptation to label it the way I just did, as *Saddam's* genocide, even among my people. I have been unable to completely avoid it, even this book. There is always that temptation to say that it was his fault, and his fault alone. Why is that temptation there? The first and most obvious reason is that Saddam Hussein *did* play a huge role in ordering massacres of my people. In a dictatorship where he and his family had such direct control over the armed forces, it is impossible for things to have been otherwise. We also have his famous statement that the eight thousand men and boys taken from around Erbil "betrayed the country and went to Hell because of it," as evidence of his knowledge of what was going on. I don't think anyone disputes that Saddam was at the heart of the genocide against my people, even when they seem determined to officially ignore the fact that it was a genocide.

Another reason for this tendency is because it is neat, and people tend to seek neat, easy explanations for things. Saddam's evil makes for a convenient explanation. One that doesn't involve asking awkward questions about how many other people were involved in the process of the genocide or about what they might be doing now. In the same way, as we have seen in chapter eight, there was a tendency in history books immediately following World War Two to blame Hitler and just a small portion of the Nazi party for the Jewish Holocaust, the war, and every other evil occurring in Germany at the time, rather than admitting the full extent of the support for and involvement in those policies.

The obvious advantage of doing this is that it simplifies any process of reconciliation. It makes for a convenient ending thanks to Saddam's trial and execution, a way of saying that the man behind it all is dead, so why do people need to look any more closely at what happened? That reduces the possibility for future conflict or the politics of revenge, thus helping to speed the process of producing stability in Iraq. It also means that local officials or army members who might have been complicit in the process of the genocide are able to continue function-ing in administrative roles in the south of the country.

In effect, it creates a version of history that serves as a uniting force in Iraq. It creates the story of everybody being in it together against Saddam, rather than large portions of the population actively supporting and working for him through one of the most brutal periods of his regime. I can understand why governments might want to promote that version of history in the interests of stability, but it also means that genuinely culpable people might not be brought to justice. More than sixty-five years after the end of the Second World War, there are still individuals being put on trial for their involvement in atrocities. Less than a decade after the fall of Saddam, it seems that all hopes of justice for those killed in the Anfal, Halabja, and the rest of the on-going campaign against the Kurds are gone.

It even seems to be one of the reasons why there is no desire in many governments to officially recognise what happened to my people as genocide. Saddam, it must be remembered, was not tried for his actions against my people, but for the murder of a small group of Shi'ite Muslims early in his reign. Nor have there been official investigations since. Effectively, with Saddam dead, people have tried to declare the matter closed. This was not absolute, of course. Ali Hasan Al Majid (Chemical Ali) *was* tried and executed in relation to Halabja, but there seems to be little official will to prosecute those who acted at lower levels.

The dangers in all this are numerous. First, it says that the suffering of the Kurds under Saddam is effectively a minor matter, easily dealt with on the legal level. Yet we can see from genocides elsewhere that they leave scars and resentments for many years, and need to be properly addressed if they are not to have knock-on effects for decades to come. Secondly, it tells those considering genocide elsewhere that while there might be repercussions for those in charge of them if they have also angered the international community in other ways, in general, a genocide alone will not be enough to bring down the wrath of outside nations. Thirdly, it means that as Iraq is rebuilt, individuals who previously helped out with the genocide against my people may come to be in positions of authority again. Unless we also subscribe to the idea that it was all down to Saddam, that is a very worrying possibility for the safety of Kurdistan.

In terms of understanding what happened, the emphasis on Saddam can also cause problems. Because of the focus Saddam, people often don't stop to consider the wider factors that went into producing the genocide. That means that it will be harder to recognise those factors if they ever arise again, and it is also hard to fully understand the context of what happened. In particular, the focus on Saddam and what he did means that there is a lack of focus on the international community and what it failed to do. There is consequently a lack of understanding of how the genocide in Kurdistan fits into a wider international context.

It even causes problems simply in terms of the way Kurdistan wishes to be perceived. By focusing on Saddam, Kurdistan is turned into a footnote to his life, when it should be so much more than that. It means that events in the region from 1970 onwards are seen effectively through the lens of Saddam, rather than in terms of the courage and resilience of the Kurdish people.

So, if we accept that the genocide wasn't *solely* down to the evil of Saddam, what was it down to? We have seen in the chapter on genocides elsewhere that, while we cannot ascribe simplistic causes to such events, they

frequently happen in situations where a group
has been separated out from society, where there
is a history of conflict between that group and
others, where there is a sufficiently authoritarian state to coerce people into taking part in the
genocide, where there are outside stresses on
that state, and frequently, when there are crises
in the state that can be conveniently ascribed to
a group.

From what we have seen throughout this
book, it seems clear that the majority of these
elements applied in the case of Kurdistan. Was
there a separation between Kurds and the rest
of society? The answer to that is obviously
yes. The Kurds represent a very distinct ethnic
group, with their own language and culture
separate from that of the largely Arabic south
of the country. My people were and are present
in a largely well-defined area of the country,
making it easy to point to them on a map as a
target. Even the mountains that have protected
the Kurds for so long may not have helped
with this, because they help to create a sense of
separation from the centre.

Moreover, my people rightly take pride
in being Kurdish, and even in countries that
persecute them are unlikely to give up their
sense of identity. Why should they, though,
when countries such as Turkey have at times
refused to even recognize their existence? If the

Kurds do not make the effort to say that they are Kurds and proud of that identity, who else will? Yet that same sense of identity probably made it easier for Saddam's regime to identify them as something separate to be blamed and dealt with, by any means necessary.

We have also seen that there is a clear history of conflict between the Kurds and, not just Iraq, but many of the surrounding countries. Particularly dangerously, in terms of factors leading to genocide, this has been a conflict about their separate identity, and especially the desire of my people to establish a homeland in which to live without being controlled by the Turkish or Arab rulers who have dictated their fates for more than a century now.

When I provided a brief history of the Kurds in chapter one, I argued for the dangers of seeing Kurdish struggles for independence as being interconnected, rather than as a distinct series of reactions to injustices, on the basis that it creates the impression that the Kurds are in a state of perpetual revolt. In other words, it presents them as a permanent problem to be solved in an equally permanent way. In many ways, this attitude is precisely the one many of those in authority within Iraq seem to have possessed. Even Saddam's quote about the fate of the eight thousand men and boys murdered by his troops seems to point to that attitude, portraying my people as being inherently 'traitors' after the separatist violence of the early 1970s.

Of course, there is a danger in this that we end up almost blaming the Kurds for what happened to them if we focus too strongly on the history of violence between them and the regime. Yet that is certainly not my intention, and it should be remembered that, however much they may have couched them, or even seen them, in terms of eliminating the Kurds' ability to rebel, the actions of the Iraqi regime were just as frequently targeted at civilians including women and children as at actively combatant men. Indeed, chemical attacks such as that at Halabja actually had a higher rate of fatalities among the young and the elderly. I am not trying to present any genocide as somehow 'reasonable' here, but merely attempting to show why the one in Kurdistan could have come to pass.

The next element that is typically found as a precursor to genocide is an orderly or authoritarian regime, because only such a regime possesses the organisational capacity to murder its citizens on a large scale. The applicability of this element to Saddam Hussein's Iraq should be obvious. It was a dictatorship, where even if we cannot ascribe every act to Saddam personally, he certainly held overall control of the running of the state. His close allies and family handled those aspects to which he could not attend personally, and the whole country was designed to run efficiently from the top down. With a large and tightly organised army, Saddam certainly had the political and military structures in place that represent a warning sign when it comes to genocide.

Were there stresses on the state and/or crises to precipitate the genocide? We can see quite clearly that there were, in the form of at least two main strands. The first was conflict with Iran. It seems to have been the case over at least the last thirty years that whenever Iran and Iraq have argued, the Kurds have found themselves caught in the middle. Iran has sought to use my people as a way to destabilize its neighbour, while Iraq has pushed the Kurds closer to Iran through its repression.

On several occasions, repression from the regime has come either in the wake of conflict with Iran, where Saddam has blamed *all* Kurds for those who chose to side with Iran, or in the context of on-going conflict with Iran. Saddam's first wave of repression against the Kurds, for example, came in the wake of the 1975 peace agreement between the two countries. An agreement that, as we have seen, effectively left the Kurds to fend for themselves.

By these criteria, it seems that the events in Kurdistan from 1970 onwards clearly contained the possibility of future violence. All the signs were there, yet it seems that the international community ignored those signs. The countries around Iraq did not protest at the treatment of my people, and nor did those further off with positions of influence on the international stage, such as the USA, those in Europe, the USSR or China.

Perhaps we can answer that by pointing out that these conditions exist in a number of regions worldwide. Dictators and marginalised ethnic groups are both woefully common, while pressures and crises are equally frequent over any long period of history. Perhaps we could argue that it is impossible for people to interfere in every such case, simply because the numbers of them mean that those attempting to help would never be able to stop. Perhaps it is also legitimate to say that while the majority of genocides share similar precursors, the mere presence of those elements does not automatically mean that genocide will follow.

Yet even if we accept that, we still have to ask why nations outside Iraq chose to continue to ignore what was happening, even after Saddam's troops started to murder the Kurds. They ignored the forcible relocation of whole villages and the effective creation of prison camps through the use of 'prohibited' areas. They ignored the mass murder of men and boys in 1983. They ignored on-going repression and the beginnings of the Anfal campaign. They even largely ignored Halabja, because while the use of chemical weapons against the Kurds was cited as a reason for intervention in Iraq in the early 1990s, it certainly wasn't the main reason. Country after country seems to have ignored what was happening in Iraq, either deliberately or through a more general lack of interest. How did that happen?

Inevitably, the answer is far from neat. It varies both according the country in question and at least a little according to the time period. Let's take two places that might conceivably have been expected to pay attention to what was happening in Kurdistan due to their Kurdish populations first: Turkey and Syria. Why did these two countries not have anything to say about a genocide happening just over their borders, and even driving refugees into their countries?

One reason is that they have terrible human rights records of their own to contend with. In theory, Turkey's attempts to join the European Union mean that it now has a much greater commitment to human rights than it used to have, but certainly in the 1980s and 1990s, there were significant human rights abuses going on. Syria, meanwhile, continues to have very little respect for the rights and well-being of

those people living within it. Neither would
have wanted to draw attention to human rights
abuses and repression in another country, for
fear of bringing similar scrutiny to bear on
themselves.

Their attitudes to the Kurds, meanwhile,
were in many ways little better than those in
Iraq. Syrian Kurds were (and are) subjected
to numerous acts of violence and repression,
including arbitrary arrest and torture. Turkey,
meanwhile, refused to even admit the existence of the Kurds as a separate ethnic group.
It banned the speaking of Kurdish, and many
Turkish officials continue to refuse to acknowledge Kurdistan's existence. I have found this
last point out personally several times while
passing through Turkey on the way to Kurdistan,
when airport officials inevitably pretend not to
understand where it is, and make a point of
insisting that I am flying to Iraq, because there
is "no such place" as Kurdistan.

Both of these elements do a lot to explain why
neither country was ever likely to pay attention
to the suffering of my people in Iraq. Yet there
is one final reason, which is that many of the
leaders of those countries have had more in
common with one another. Again and again
in their histories through this period, we see
leaders with western educations, military and
a certain distance from their own populations.

They were actually in a better position in many ways to feel sympathy for Saddam than for those he ordered massacred.

We cannot say the same for Iran. Decades of conflict with Iraq, coupled with leaders with almost diametrically opposed international connections, would seem to make Iran the perfect place to speak out against, and even act against, the Iraqi genocide. Iran has used the Kurds in its conflicts against Iraq on several occasions, moreover. It should have been perfect. Indeed, it is to Iran that many members of my family fled in the early days of the oppression against the Kurds, and to which I eventually escaped.

Yet there was never a feeling that Iran particularly wanted us there. Part of that is religious. The majority of Kurds are Sunni Muslims, while Iran is predominantly Shi'ite. Part of it is simply the antipathy many nations feel to large groups of refugees who need to be protected and housed. Large parts of it must be down to the authoritarian nature of its own regime, and the difficulty of it therefore commenting on human rights abuses elsewhere.

Probably more of it, though, was about Iran's on again, off again conflict with Iraq over territory, as well as the role Iran saw for the Kurds in that conflict. It had two main effects. The first was to make it very difficult for Iran to interfere in any of Iraq's affairs even if it wanted to.

Iraq was unlikely to bow to pressure to Iran on any issue, and Iran has been demonstrably unwilling to prolong or adjust its wars with Iraq to protect the Kurds. Proof of this can be found in the 1975 Algiers Agreement that effectively abandoned Kurdistan once Iran got what it wanted from Iraq. Even though the Iran-Iraq war was on-going, it was not likely to take additional military risks to protect the Kurds.

In any case, the Kurds are not a people for whom Iran feels any genuine friendship. Instead, it has been the case time and time again that Iran has sought to use my people as a means of destabilising Iraq, either to limit Iraq's ability to pose a threat to Iran, or in support of Iran's own conflicts with it.

For Iran, the Kurds have been a way to fight Iraq *without* fighting Iraq. In fact, it could be argued that rather than doing anything to help Kurdistan, Iran's emphasis on it as a weapon against Iraq was part of what put my people in danger in the first place.

It was certainly never going to act militarily to save my people's lives, even if peshmerga were able to operate from the Iranian side of the border, making forays into Iraq before returning to relative safety in Iran.

So it seems clear why many of those neighbouring countries with large populations of Kurds did not help.

What about countries farther afield? What about those in Europe that were so quick to claim interests in Iraq and the surrounding countries when they were formed in the 1920s?

Can we claim that they had no knowledge of what was going on? Certainly, European countries did not receive the waves of Kurdish refugees that Iran, Syria and Turkey did, but it seems unreasonable to suggest that they were unaware of the atrocities being committed. International organisations such as Human Rights Watch and Amnesty International commented clearly on them, and presumably it cannot have been too difficult for leaders in France, Germany (with its large Kurdish population) or the UK to have read their reports.

Was there the will to act? We can see from the involvement of several European countries in the eventual Iraq wars that there was a will to act in some quarters, yet it seems not to have been sustained or general. France, for example, has been much more opposed to action in Iraq than several other European countries. There is a temptation to ascribe this unwillingness to a desire to keep oil flowing, and that kind of economic consideration must certainly have played a role, yet I suspect that a lot of it was down to a feeling that Iraq's affairs were a long way away and nothing to do with them. It may even have had something to do with a post-colonial unwillingness to exert authority over other areas of the world, for fear of being seen as arrogant Europeans imposing their will on other countries.

Or could it be that they simply didn't have the power to act? Certainly, Europe's influence in the Middle East is much less than it was in the days between the wars, and militarily, many European countries do not have the ability to act alone that they once did. Yet the very fact that combined international forces were eventually able to topple Saddam suggests that they were in a position to do something. If not singly, then acting through the UN.

Yet it is here that we hit a problem, because the UN is no less culpable in ignoring this genocide than anyone else. Indeed, the UN's primary tactic when faced with human rights abuses and even genocide the world over seems to be to stand back and either ignore or ineffectually condemn it, all the while carefully avoiding the word genocide. The reasons for this are obvious. It is composed of so many countries with conflicting interests that actually getting a UN resolution, let alone action to back it up, is next to impossible.

The influence of Russia/the USSR and China on this should not be underestimated. Both countries are members of the UN security-council, along with the UK, France and USA, with the power of veto. They shared many of the human rights issues of Kurdistan's neighbours, and thus an unwillingness to make those issues the basis for intervention in a country.

The USSR's overarching influence in the region may also have had a role to play. It sought to build strong relations with both Iran and Iraq (though the US also sought influence in those countries to counter it) and so tended to support the actions of the regimes, even coming to strongly support Iraq in the Iran-Iraq war of 1980-1988. As such, it was unlikely to undermine a relationship with an ally by intervening in Iraq's genocidal campaigns.

More than that, because of the closeness of Iraq to several regions of the USSR, Moscow is likely to have been very wary of outside intervention in the country. Particularly American intervention. Evidence for this can be seen in the slow slide of America towards war with Iraq following the collapse of the Soviet Union. Only as the USSR became less able to exert pressure against action in the Middle East did war become possible.

Its Cold War relations with the USSR were clearly one reason why the USA chose not to stop the genocide during the 1980s, as the imposition of the no-fly zone in the 1990s demonstrates. Yet there were almost certainly other reasons for it as well. The US desire for stability in the Middle

East cannot be underestimated as a factor here. A stable Iraq and Iran balancing one another was a more desirable situation for America than one dominating the other. America's policies in South America have shown that it is more than willing to work with dictators in the name of 'stability', so why should that not have been the case here? We can even see that need for balance in the USA's reaction to Halabja, when it pushed for a UN resolution requiring *both* Iran and Iraq to refrain from the use of chemical weapons, despite knowing that Iran had not used them.[16]

Although it can be hard to remember when the US has been embroiled in foreign wars for over a decade, there was also a general American unwillingness to risk direct military action for many years. America has historically had a disinclination towards foreign interventions, from the Monroe doctrine's insistence on avoiding interference in Europe's colonies elsewhere to the time it took to become involved in conflicts such as World War Two. More recently, the Vietnam War in particular convinced the USA to avoid involvement in apparently minor foreign conflicts, because of the danger of losses to US lives. Politically, such losses were seen as impossible to tolerate.

That is not to say that the USA avoided interference in Iraq and the surrounding region.

16   Hiltermann, pp183-205

As we have previously seen, its support for Iran in the early 1970s played a key role in persuading the Kurds to rise up against Saddam's Iraq, while its role in brokering the 1975 Algiers Accord arguably sparked much of the earliest oppression of my people under Saddam. I have referred previously to Henry Kissinger's statement that "covert action should not be confused with missionary work", which shows quite clearly one of the main reasons America did not get involved. The USA's primary concern was its own interests, and until the 1990s, helping the Kurds did not coincide with them. Certainly, this helps to explain the gap between the rhetoric of Saddam's evil and the point where action was finally taken.

So, there are clear reasons why people outside Iraq chose to ignore what was happening in Kurdistan. I suppose it might even be reasonable to ask whether we have any right to expect that someone from outside *should* have tried to intervene. The argument generally runs that to stop such a thing you would have to go to war, and that bombing a country to save its people is an oxymoron. Yet I have to ask whether that is really a valid argument. Can we really justify standing by in cases where we know that civilians are being systematically killed?

In the case of Kurdistan in particular, we are not talking about a major intervention.

The majority of work on the ground in Kurdistan was done by my people, not by outside forces. The provision of the no-fly zone helped to level the playing field against an oppressor with significant technological advantages, but the Kurds were not asking to be saved. They were looking for an opportunity to save themselves.

What is slightly worrying here is the extent to which the genocide in Iraq continues to be ignored. Some countries, most recently the UK, recognise the genocide now, along with key organisations, but there is still a considerable lack of attention given to what happened. Although over, its history should still be a crucial part of understanding recent events in the region, yet even among those who know about it, it seems to be increasingly reduced to a kind of shorthand, with a focus on Halabja, perhaps the Anfal, but mostly the fall of Saddam. Presumably the argument there is that it is over, but remembrance is vital in cases such as this.

Perhaps the reasons for the lack of remembrance are similar to the ones for not getting involved in the first place. There is still substantial hatred for the Kurds in some quarters, and there are still regimes that do not want to suggest that an appropriate response to a murderous regime might be to overthrow it. Other countries, meanwhile, might not want to remember the extended period for which they stood by, allowing the genocide to continue. Alternatively, they might be reluctant to emphasise the precedent that it poses, where they are potentially morally obliged to intervene wherever mass murder is taking place, because of the risk it creates of being constantly involved in foreign wars. Even simple academic interest may have a role to play here, with other areas of the Iraq war providing far simpler avenues for exploration.

It may also be that continued forgetfulness about the genocide in Iraq is a deliberate effort to achieve the same quality that may have contributed to many countries ignoring it in the first place. Stability. I have suggested above that the focus on Saddam has meant that there have not been the range of prosecutions for the genocide that have followed in areas such as the Balkans, for example. Yet it seems likely that at least partly, this is to avoid the divisive effects of a lengthy process of identifying further culprits, in an Iraq that is, aside from Kurdistan, still far from stable.

Should we place this apparently elusive quality of 'stability' above the truth? Is there not a danger, in a country prepared to forget its own crimes, that they could repeat themselves? More generally, we have to ask whether similar crimes could take place unobserved and not acted upon in the future in the way they did in Kurdistan. The answers to that are not simple, because we know that massacres and attempted genocides have taken place elsewhere in the world. The horrors of Sudan make it clear that this is not a phenomenon confined to the Kurds. Worse, in Sudan we find that there was the same unwillingness or inability on the part of the international community to protect civilians in many cases.

In Libya, we can see that international support of the kind offered to Kurdistan was available when its people wanted to overthrow Colonel Gadhafi, yet the international community has been much slower to intervene in Syria, despite reports of the government shelling its own people. Large sections of the American political elite, meanwhile, continue to press for the earliest possible withdrawal from Iraq, in language that makes it clear they want to avoid similar foreign wars wherever possible in future. Indeed, if another Saddam were to perpetrate the same genocide in Kurdistan five years from now, it seems likely that my people would have just as little support from outside Iraq.

Worse, we know that the conditions for genocide discussed above continue to exist in many of those countries Kurds make their homes. Countries such as Syria continue to function under authoritarian regimes facing challenges and crises in the form of revolts and international pressure. Kurds live within them and are readily identifiable group that has a history of conflict with the regime. At the time of writing, the situation in Syria has already progressed to civil war, and the Kurds there could soon find themselves in a precarious position. If they do, will they find the support and aid they need to survive? Or will they find themselves abandoned for too long while they are killed?

The truth is that we do not know, but the history of what happened in Kurdistan makes for worrying reading in that context. Although Kurdistan is thriving now, and has received considerable international assistance, at the moment when it mattered most, it found the people in a position to help it standing by, either unaware or unwilling to help.

10

Looking back to move ahead

I have tried to do a lot in this book. I have
tried to give a personal account of some of the
worst events in Iraq's history, while still giving
enough of their broader sweep to allow the
reader to truly understand them. I have tried
to step back and explore the factors influencing
events, while staying close enough to make it
clear that these were people's lives being taken
from them, and that real people were suffering. I have tried to go further with the Anfal
by connecting it to the past as part of one long
programme of genocide by the regime, placing
it in the context of other genocides around the
globe and exploring why no one intervened in
it while it was happening. I have also tried to
show some of the ways in which Kurdistan has
rebuilt itself, as well as some of the obstacles
to that rebuilding. Kurdistan should be about
so much more than the genocide perpetrated
against it.

Yet if there is one message I want to leave you
with, it is this: what happened in Kurdistan
under Saddam Hussein's regime was genocide.
It was an attempt to wipe out, partially or

completely, the Kurdish people. It must not be forgotten.

That claim does not seem like such a difficult one to accept. In the face of the closest thing to the tactics of the holocaust since Nazi Germany, it is hard to see how the world could not accept it. Yet much of it does not. The human rights court of The Hague *has* declared the Anfal a genocide, but the British government, the government of the country I now call home, and which has so many other freedoms, has only just officially acknowledged the genocide as such, twenty-five years after the Anfal. Many other countries around the world, who would otherwise denounce genocide and violence in general terms, continue to deny that it was genocide completely.

There are reasons for that continued denial, including the refusal to acknowledge the obligation it would have owed the Kurds and the precedent it would set for any similar scale and type of conflict in the future. It holds to what Shaw describes as the impossible standard of the Holocaust[17] because it is not currently politically expedient for any country to do anything else, yet I hope that the case for a genocide having occurred in Kurdistan is clear by now.

Chapter one showed us the roots of that

17   Martin Shaw, What is Genocide
(Polity Press, 2007)

genocide in the recent history of Kurdistan and Iraq. It argued that seeing multiple Kurdish attempts to carve out a homeland as part of one on-going conflict made it easy for the rulers of Iraq to see my people as a problem to be solved rather than as people with legitimate concerns and needs. It also suggested that Saddam Hussein's involvement in the failed peace agreement of 1970 may have contributed either to him taking on that view of the Kurds as a problem to be solved in increasingly violent ways, or as something to be hated and wiped out. Which of these was the case does not ultimately matter, and both views are likely to have been present to some extent among the wide range of people involved in the genocide.

Chapter two showed what I believe to be the first steps along a path that led to genocide, with the clearing of villages and the imprisonment of many of my people, including myself. These first steps showed how Saddam's regime was willing to break with the past through the use of large scale imprisonment in camps, and I argued that they should be seen as connected to the rest of the genocide, on the basis that it cannot be fully understood without them.

Chapter three explored what life was like in the camps, emphasising that conditions were part of an on-going process designed to contain and ultimately destroy us. It also focussed on one of the first mass killings of my people under Saddam, in the form of the murder of 8,000 Barzani men and boys taken from the camps. I argued that this killing should be seen as fundamentally connected to what came five years later, as an escalation of violence towards my people in the next step along a path of genocide.

Chapter four examined the Anfal, looking at its stages, its intentions, and its effects. I asked whether there was any legitimate way the murder of up to 182,000 of my people could not be considered a genocide, and I sought to connect it to previous events to show that it formed part of an on-going programme of destruction aimed at my people, rather than some one-off event that could be dismissed as anything less.

Chapter five looked at the most well-known event of the Anfal: the bombing of Halabja. There, I argued that Halabja shouldn't be seen as something separate, while showing the ways in which the regime's propaganda campaign operated even during its genocide of my people, deflecting blame, confusing the issue and persuading even those targeted by the attacks that Saddam's regime was not to blame.

Chapter six explored the events of 1991 and how the regime's continuing repression came to an end. It showed that even as we escaped it,

Saddam's regime sought to destroy my people, but also argued against his repression in other areas doing anything to damage the claim of genocide against my people.

Chapter seven explored the rebuilding of Kurdistan, along with the civil war. It showed some of the ways in which Kurdistan is remaking itself from day to day, and explored some of the factors influencing the astonishing speed of the transformation it is undergoing at the present time. It also explored how these same factors have influenced the shape of that transformation, and in particular the prioritising of immediate physical reconstruction projects in the early period of the rebuilding.

Chapter eight tried to place the genocide in Kurdistan in its proper context. It took examples of other genocides from around the world, looking at their methods and the factors that produced them. I made two key points there: that other well-known genocides are consistent with what happened to my people under Saddam's regime, and that even many of those are either not legally defined as genocides, or were not defined as such at the time, because 'genocide' requires action, with the result that the term genocide has become almost impossible to apply in any realistic way.

In chapter nine, I looked at this further, as well as exploring the responses of countries around

Kurdistan to the genocide. I looked at how much the world knew at the time, at why there has been, and continues to be, so little known about it, and at the extent to which the world was effectively complicit in what happened to my people. I also explored the extent to which, by thinking of this as being about Saddam, we have robbed my people of justice or given the world a license to ignore events.

In all, I have sought to first explore the genocide in Kurdistan in broader terms than is usually done, arguing for its continuity with their whole repression by the regime. That is important. I feel that we cannot fully understand any genocide without looking at its context, and that looking at only the Anfal, while seemingly like the logical thing to do, actually reduces our understanding of it.

The Iraqi regime did not just wake up one day in 1988 and decide to eliminate my people. Instead, the Anfal must be understood as simply the most serious step taken along a path that Saddam Hussein's supporters were on from at least 1970. It was a path aimed ultimately at the destruction of the Kurdish people, either from simple hatred or as a murderous extension of the stabilising instincts of counter-insurgency. It was a path that the regime proceeded along in demonstrable steps, either as their previous ones failed to 'solve' the 'problem' of the Kurds, or as its position allowed it to proceed further with its violence.

I firmly believe that the Anfal was not the last step in that process. It removed my people from rural areas, concentrating them either in camps or cities, while reducing their ability to defend themselves, but looking back, it does not seem like a last step. Instead, it seems more like a preparation, one aimed at making it easy to finally destroy my people as and when it became either 'necessary' or simply possible.

Looked at like that, I believe that I have been very lucky in some ways. So many people I knew did not make it out of the camps. I have lost friends and family both to Saddam's regime and to the civil war in Kurdistan. I have been thrown back by those taking men and boys to die when others my age were taken. I have survived conditions, both in the camps and on the march to safety beyond Iraq's borders, that killed others.

My story is inherently caught up with that of this genocide. I was born near its start, and I was there when it ended. I spent time imprisoned by the regime, and I was there when we escaped. I have seen Kurdistan rise up afterwards, too, rebuilding itself in ways that most countries could not after so much damage. I have tried to give the reader my recollections here, because sometimes the only thing someone can add to a story is to say that they were there. I was there, and I know what happened.

I know what has happened since the genocide too, and I have tried to focus on that here as well. While the genocide must not be forgotten, Kurdistan deserves to be remembered for more than that. It needs to be celebrated for the speed of its recovery and acknowledged as one of the few stable regions in an often turbulent country. Currently, there are those in the region who call it a second Dubai, but at the same time, there are plenty of people in the world who haven't heard of Kurdistan at all, or if they have, they have heard only about the tensions and violence of the past. That deserves to change.

What lies next for Kurdistan? That is a complex question. If we could accurately predict the future course of a whole region, then we would have been able to avoid what Saddam's regime did. Yet at the same time, it is possible to look for signs of what might happen in the things that are happening today.

So, what *is* happening? As I write this, the region is engaged in a standoff with the south of Iraq over Kirkuk and whether it is rightfully Kurdish or Iraqi. As so often before with Kirkuk, the desire for the oil resources that come with the city have clouded questions over its Kurdish identity. Could that break out into open war? Certainly, there has been a military build-up along the borders between Kurdistan and Iraq.

This one situation says so much about how far Kurdistan has come, and how little, in other ways, things have changed. That Iraq and Kurdistan can face one another across a clear border says that Kurdistan *has* a border; that it is closer now to being a country in its own right than it has ever been. It has its own military and its own government. It speaks with Iraq's government essentially the way a separate state would, being one in all but name.

Perhaps this crisis will be the push that causes Kurdistan to finally declare its independence. Perhaps the world is ready to accept it as a separate country. Possibly, in Kurdistan, the world is getting a lesson in the way countries really come into being. Not through the formal creation of Great Powers intent on carving up the world as happened at the start of the twenti-eth century, but through people carving out their own space in the region they have lived for many thousands of years.

Could Kurdistan be a separate country? It has everything in place that it might need politically, socially and economically. Politically, it has a functioning parliament that is arguably more democratic than any other in the surround-ing region. It has an unusual but time proven structure of governance through the parties in the cities and provinces. It has a functioning and effective police force, and an army that has stood against some of the most dangerous opponents surrounding Kurdistan.

Socially and economically, Kurdistan has made great strides in the last two decades. It is a wealthier region now than it has ever been, with access to important natural resources and a society that has started to get over the effects of large amounts of its people being displaced enough to have a definite sense of identity in the region. Not only is it in a position to become a nation, but it has the potential to be a wealthier, fairer, better run nation than almost any of those around it.

Kurdistan is in a position where many other countries relate to it as a nation. The US has received its ambassadors, while countries seeking oil now have to deal with it directly. It has done what is historically the most difficult job of an emerging nation, which is to create the *idea* of itself as a nation. It probably says a lot about how ready Kurdistan is to be a sovereign state that if the UN were to turn around and acknowledge it as such tomorrow, very little would need to change.

Yet how likely is that to happen in the near future? Iraq seems to be vehemently opposed to Kurdistan leaving it, or at least to losing the resources it represents. At the same time, those countries with an interest in rebuilding Iraq, including the US, may feel that Kurdistan leaving would destabilise it at just the point where it needs to hold together the most. I am not sure whether that is actually true, because Kurdistan has been so separate from it in all but name for years that it would make little practical difference, but in these things, the symbol often counts for more than the reality.

Most of Kurdistan's neighbours would be opposed to any move towards independence too. Iran, Turkey and Syria all have borders with Kurdistan, as explained in the introduction, and all have Kurdish populations. Most of them have mistreated those populations repeatedly in the past decades. Worse, several have on-going conflicts within their countries with Kurdish separatist groups. As such, they must be terrified of the possibility of Kurdistan becoming an independent country, because of the risk that regions of their own countries would want to break away and join it over time.

Whether that would actually be likely to happen, I don't know. Kurdistan has always been clear about its ambitions and about the limits of those ambitions. Its government has made it clear on several occasions that it is not seeking the kind of larger Kurdistan some people seem to fear coming into existence. Moreover, I cannot see the international community accepting the secession of whole provinces from other countries any time soon after the formation of Kurdistan as a state.

Yet even if it did happen, would it necessarily be such a bad thing? Those countries awarded portions of Kurdistan by the Great Powers in the early twentieth century have long complained of difficulties with their Kurdish populations. Allowing them to join the country of their choosing might actually ease some of the pressures on the countries that have repressed them to date.

Realistically though, in the present climate, it seems unlikely that the UN would acknowledge Kurdistan. With the countries around it so unsettled, and with Syria actually in the middle of a civil war, it would probably never risk further destabilising the region. In any case, there are currently other regions, such as Palestine, demanding statehood in the face of severe opposition. Many people might oppose Kurdistan's acknowledgement as a state just to avoid setting a precedent. Though that works both ways. If Palestine should become a separate state, then that surely strengthens the case for Kurdistan?

It is hard to say whether that will come to pass at this point. It is difficult to say with certainty whether there is even the political will inside Kurdistan to push for nationhood at the moment. The PDK remain committed to it as a goal, but the PUK appear to be content to work within the context of an Iraq without excessive controls over the region. Possibly, the increased tensions with the Iraqi government will change that, but it is impossible to be sure, and a project such as nationhood really needs cross party support if it is not to risk tearing Kurdistan apart again.

On one level though, the increasing militarisation of the argument over Kirkuk with the Iraqi government is actually a good sign for nationhood. If Bagdad is trying to secure control of the city and take it outside of Kurdistan then there must be a reason. Bagdad has always wanted Kirkuk, but why act *now*? Assuming it is not simply greed for the city's wealth, then it is most likely to be about securing Kirkuk as a part of Iraq in the event that Kurdistan secedes from the country. Attempting to force the issue of Kirkuk is almost an acknowledgement that a separate Kurdistan with no control from Bagdad cannot be far away.

If Kurdistan does become independent, then I will celebrate. I will celebrate a world where my people finally have a place that they can call their own, living according to their own political will and not that of an Arab majority not interested in them except as troublesome rebels. I will celebrate the success of a project that so many of my people have died in the service of.

For the moment though, I am worried. I am worried that perhaps the current crisis will be the one that starts the violence again. Because that is the danger. This book has been a history of events, a collection of my opinions, a kind of memoir of some of the worst moments in Iraq's history, and everything here shows how easily things could slide over into more violence against my people. If I am adamant that Kurdistan must be free, it is because the only alternative seems to be the death and repression of my people.

In this book, we have seen the elements that pushed Kurdistan into crisis and sent Iraqi forces murdering my people in the past, from unsettled borders, to uprisings, to continued conflict over Kurdistan's resources. We have seen in general terms that genocides often come out of situations where we have the aftermath of unstable situations, but an increasingly ordered state looking for someone to blame for its troubles, or when persecuted minorities want to break away from larger states that want to hold onto the territory they occupy.

Those are the same things that apply today. Kurdistan is currently attached to an unsettled state in the form of Iraq, which is trying to assert its unity and identity just as Kurdistan is looking to push for separation. There is a strong history of conflict between them, and probably also a desire on the part of the Iraqi government to ensure that none of its neighbours gain an advantage from a separate Kurdistan. There is also a desire on the part of both that government and Kurdistan's not to be seen to be weak.

So yes, the conditions exist for violence to erupt once more in Kurdistan, if not now, then at some point further into the future. I wish that were not the case, but we cannot ignore the dangers of a situation such as the one Kurdistan is in. Worse, the conditions exist for that violence to spill over into genocide. Not just in terms of the political pressures on the Iraqi government, but also in terms of the kind of war that would be likely to result if conflict did come about. Because, as we have seen before, the line between counter insurgency and genocide can be a blurred one, especially in Iraq.

I sincerely hope that it never comes to that, but if it does, can we expect anyone to stop it? In fact, let's move that question away from the emotive issue of Kurdistan for a moment to ask a more general question. If there were another genocide on the scale of the one in Kurdistan tomorrow, would anyone hear about it? Would anyone *do* anything about it? If not, why not?

From what we saw in chapters eight and nine, I have to say that the answer is probably that the world would do nothing. It would hear about it, because despite the efforts of regimes around the world to hide their genocides, we have evidence of them today. Evidence that was generally available at the time, making it clear to governments around the world what was happening. From Kurdistan to Bosnia and Sudan, we have the evidence, and we had it at the time.

But what would be done? Even today, even after everything that has gone before, if there were another genocide in Kurdistan, the likelihood is that the world would do nothing. If there were a genocide in the context of some future war with Iraq, there might be a diplomatic response, and probably diplomatic efforts made to persuade both sides to negotiate, but that would achieve little. It might actually drive any violence forward quicker, so as to achieve the maximum amount before any ceasefire, in the same way that the Anfal proceeded at a furious pace and concluded before any censure could finally take root.

There would almost certainly be no direct intervention in such a genocide, despite the presence of foreign forces in Iraq. Yes, the US intervened minimally when Iraq became involved in the Kurdish civil war, using cruise missiles at a distance and organising evacuations. Yes, its current presence in Iraq shows a new willingness to intervene in the world directly, but it still seems unlikely that they would do anything. If the 2003 war in

Iraq has done anything to America and many other military powers around the world, it has reaffirmed the dangers of becoming involved in conflicts beyond their borders.

What, if anything, would the UN do in the event of another genocide? We know from chapter eight that its troops have been forced to stand by in the context of genocides (or at least 'ethnic cleansing') before. We know that the differing views on the security council makes it practically impossible for it to authorise military intervention, even to save civilian lives. At best, in the event of another genocide in Kurdistan or elsewhere, it seems likely that the UN might try to establish 'safe' areas, and they have failed too many times before.

There might not even be sufficient censure after the fact for those involved. In Rwanda, the Tutsi government chose to issue a general amnesty to heal some of the wounds between the Tutsi and Hutu people, but that was its choice to make, and in any case, the nature of that genocide made it almost too general to successfully prosecute. The same cannot be said in other cases. While individuals are put on trial for war crimes, it is not for the crime of genocide even in the majority of cases that deserve it. Slobodan Milosevic, Charles Taylor and more were convicted of lesser crimes. Even if their sentences were the same as they would otherwise have been, that is an insult to their victims.

Which brings us back to Saddam Hussein and his crimes one final time. He was never convicted of any crime against the Kurds. *Any* crime. 182,000 of my people died thanks to a regime he claimed direct and total control over. He actively ordered the continuation of the Anfal. He openly condemned my people as traitors and said that he knew they went to hell when asked what had become of the men taken in 1983.

Yet he was never forced to stand trial for those crimes. He was never put on trial for genocide. Ali Hassan Al-Majid was, and was executed for it, but Saddam Hussein was instead tried for the murder of 142 shi'ites from Dujail and executed for that crime against humanity. Although clearly an evil act and one deserving justice, giving justice to the 142 dead in this cast meant denying it to hundreds of thousands of others, both in Kurdistan and elsewhere.

In an effort to quell divisions in Iraq by moving as quickly as possible on one crime, the courts ensured that the others would never be properly addressed. At the very least, there should be an official acknowledgement of the genocidal nature of Saddam's crimes.

Yet I will not end this book by talking about Saddam. He does not deserve that, and neither does Kurdistan. Instead, I would like to address two things. The first is the issue of genocide in general, and how our attitudes to it need to change. The second is a final thought on how I hope Kurdistan's future will go.

When it comes to genocide, I believe that the world has set the barrier too high. I believe that, in mandating action against it, it has given countries a reason to want to avoid using the term under all circumstances. In using the Holocaust as its benchmark, moreover, the international community has chosen a benchmark for intervention that no other genocide could reasonably live up to.

Are we really saying as a world that until a country industrialises the mass murder of its citizens and the dead number in their millions, it is none of our business? Are we really saying that international troops doing their best to protect civilians should be obliged to stand by because there is no legal mandate for them to act against mere 'ethnic cleansing'? What kind of world are we creating when we define genocide so strictly that those things are true, and what does it mean for the safety of every man, woman and child around the world when their governments could turn on them with impunity?

I know why governments choose those standards. They do not want to be forced into

wars against their wishes. They do not want to
be trapped in a situation that could potentially
trigger a worldwide conflict at some point in the
future, yet surely we can come up with a better
solution than to ignore mass murder around
the world until it is too late to save anyone?
We live in a world where warfare is no longer
conducted on clear fields of battle away from
urban centres, and where civilian populations
are increasingly being seen as targets in a kind
of total war aimed at wiping out everyone on
the opposing side. In a world like that, what
happened in Kurdistan will repeat itself again
and again until we change the way we approach
genocide as a whole.

Kurdistan, I hope, will avoid being attacked
in that way again. It is not certain. As I have
said above, the situation of Kurdistan and
Iraq remains unclear, while at the same time,
there are populations of Kurds in a number of
countries that have no respect for either human
rights or their existence. What happened in Iraq
could happen in Turkey or Syria just as easily.

My hope is that a truly independent Kurdistan
will reduce that risk, by placing my people
beyond the reach of tyrants who see them as a
problem to be solved with murder. In a world
that will not act to help us, we must be strong
enough to help ourselves, and those around us.
We must do more than that. In a world that has

sought to deny Kurdistan existence for so long, we must continue the work of making it perfect, so that when people look at it in future they ask themselves why they did not recognise its independence sooner. We must show the world that some things simply cannot be destroyed.

11

Rebirth

The other chapters in this book are devoted to the history of the genocide in Kurdistan, but this one has a different intention. In it, I intend to examine the case for Kurdistan as a separate country, and argue that it should be granted sovereign status by the UN. I strongly believe that Kurdistan should be recognised as a separate country at the earliest possible opportunity, and here, I intend to explore the reasons for that. I also intend to examine some of the counter arguments that say Kurdistan should remain as part of Iraq, and suggest that they are not sufficient to warrant keeping the region from the status of a country.

Let's start with the most straightforward of all the reasons here: the majority of my people *want* an independent Kurdistan. Kurdistan's political parties work towards independence, its people seek independence, and they will continue to push for it almost regardless of what the rest of the world chooses to do. My people want their own country, have wanted it since before the creation of Iraq, and will not stop wanting it simply because it might be convenient for the rest of Iraq, or even the world, that they should.

Historically, the strength of Kurdish feeling on the subject of independence should be obvious. There have been regular rebellions since the creation of Iraq, all designed at achieving the same aims. Whether under General Mullah Mustafa Barzani or more recently, my people have frequently felt so strongly about independence that they have been prepared to fight and die to achieve it. Does anyone really think that cause has become less important now, or that the assaults on Kurdistan under Saddam will have made independence less of an issue for us?

Obviously not, yet I am sure that there will be a temptation among some readers to ask at this point whether armed struggle is really an adequate representation of the will of the majority of people. Violence is, after all, an expression of the lengths to which someone is willing to go over their beliefs, rather than of the number of people supporting them. Does the fact that my people were willing to fight in the past adequately demonstrate that a majority of them were in favour of independence?

For the past, it does not. It cannot, simply because of the nature of the evidence. We do not have poll data from the time of each revolt asking how many Kurds supported it, because no government ever asked, and if they had, I doubt anyone would have dared to answer them truthfully. In that much, I will concede, we cannot *prove* for certain that in 1970 or 1974, 1983 or 1988, the majority of Kurds would have preferred to have lived in a separate country.

Yet I think we can infer something from the nature of those revolts. All the evidence available suggests that they were popular revolts, supported by my people. People still speak with pride about their peshmerga family members. There is still a great deal of pride in those who lost family members fighting for the cause of Kurdish independence, or to protect my people from the regime's troops. That the revolts continued to happen despite increasingly inhuman reprisals from the regime suggests something about the depth of support for them. On those occasions where they achieved success, such as the victories of 1991 in freeing cities, people seem to have been quick to support the changes.

More than that, at least some sections of the Bagdad government seem to have been convinced that all Kurds were in favour of independence.

As we have seen elsewhere, Saddam's hatred of my people seems to have been based at least partly on the belief that the vast majority would never turn away from the cause of independence. That was the 'problem' that the regime tried to solve through mass murder.

When it comes to more up to date assessments of the wishes of my people, we are able to speak from a more authoritative position. There is, for example, their consistent support for political parties in favour of either strong regional autonomy or full independence, in the form of the PDK and PUK. Those two parties continue to win the majority of seats in the regional parliament, and that *must* be seen as reflecting the desires of the ordinary inhabitants of the region. We cannot have a democratic process where we then go on to ignore those wishes.

There are also the results of independent polls on the issue of independence to consider. One Gallup poll of 2004[18] suggested that more than 55% of all Kurds across Iraq favoured independence, while just 12% felt that Kurdistan should have no more independence than any other region. When the poll questioned those Kurds actually living in the region, the proportion in favour of independence rose to 75%.

A second poll of 2005,[19] claimed that 98% of those asked during the Kurdish general elections favoured independence when presented with a more straightforward in/out choice. Although this was not an official referendum, and did

18   http://www.gallup.com/poll/11995/Gallup-Poll-Iraq-Could-Kurdistan-Iraqs-Quebec.aspx
19   http://www.indybay.org/newsitems/2005/02/09/17205061.php

not include opinions from Kurds elsewhere in Iraq, it still produced a petition with more than 1.7 million signatures asking the UN for independence. A more recent but much smaller poll conducted by the Kurdistan Institute for Political Issues suggests that the majority of Kurds still favour independence.[20]

While none of these polls is definitive, taken in combination, they make the desires of my people clear. They want independence now, just as they have wanted it throughout Iraq's modern history. To ignore those wishes seems to fly in the face of the democracy that is supposedly at the heart of Iraq now. Surely, it should be up to my people to determine their own future?

The past stands in favour of an independent Kurdistan too. There may be a temptation to consider Kurdistan firmly a part of Iraq, and so something that should not be broken away from it, yet for how long has that been true? As we saw in the first chapters of this book, a hundred years ago, Iraq as we know it did not exist. It is the post-World War One creation of European Great Powers, determined to carve up the remains of the Ottoman Empire.

They did so both in the ways that were politically convenient for them, and with a large disregard for the inhabitants of the regions that they assigned to particular countries.

20   http://www.aknews.com/en/aknews/4/327676/

More than that, they did so with the idea
that specific European countries would have
elements of continuing control and influence in
the nascent states created. The inclusion of what
is now Kurdistan in Iraq was down to a combination of the British need for ease of administration, and the need to balance the region that
fell under British control against those going to
the French and the other Western powers.

Those circumstances no longer apply. The
world where there was a need for powerful
European empires to balance their interests in
the region to avoid further war has passed. Any
need that Britain had for an Iraq shaped in such
a way as to allow it to administer it easily from
afar has gone. More than that, the experience
of the Second World War shows that the efforts
were not even successful, making the reasoning
of Iraq's modern creators a dangerous one to
follow.

The pattern of Western powers creating artifi-
cial countries is one we can see in a number of
regions elsewhere, most notably in the British
rule over the whole of the Indian subcontinent
as one political unit until 1949. There, as in Iraq,
we can see the pushing together of numerous
ethnic, religious and political groups, yet today,
who could really think of Pakistan and India
ever being one nation? The divisions between
Kurdistan and Iraq are surely as deep as those

between those two neighbours, and who would sensibly have tried to keep them together when the British left?

The modern history of the world is filled with nations splitting and re-forming along lines that better suit their current political realities. Whether it is the former soviet states re-configuring themselves now that the might of the USSR is no longer there to force them into shape, South Sudan coming into existence thanks to emergency UN recognition, or simply the pressures from regions of the UK for independence from one another, this is a time where people have recognised that the future political shapes of their countries do not have to be governed by decisions made to meet the perceived needs of the past, yet it seems that the same standards are not being applied to Kurdistan.

What about Kurdistan's history prior to the First World War? There will no doubt be those who wish to point out that for long periods of that history, Kurdistan as it stands today did not exist as a single political unit, or that it was ruled under the same empires as the rest of Iraq. Those points are both true for several periods of Kurdistan's history, and I do not intend to attempt to deny them. Yet there are other elements in Kurdistan's history that suggest it *should* have independence.

The first is that the regions making up Kurdistan have been separate kingdoms on several occasions. We saw in chapter one that provinces containing Kurdistan's main cities were each ruled separately by princes prior to their absorption into the Ottoman Empire, and even under the Persians, they led at least a semi-independent existence. At no time prior to Iraq's creation were they considered a part of the same political unit as the south.

There are the links to the region's original Mesopotamian and Babylonian cultures to consider, too. As a region, Kurdistan retains links to an ancient past rich in history and culture, the Arab rulers claiming ownership of the region cannot claim the same links. Instead, the ancient history of the region is one of those rulers coming in to conquer it. That may not seem relevant now. It is. Kurdistan may be a modern country, not focussed on its ancient past, but it that past is entirely relevant if individuals outside Kurdistan start to suggest that it has somehow always been a part of Iraq.

Kurdistan's older history adds one more thing to the argument for an independent nation, which is that its people have always been seen as distinct. As we saw in chapter one, even the earliest writers referred to them separately from the rest of the Persian Empire. They were a distinct people even then, and were not, as

Turkey in particular has suggested, just a sub-set of the other ethnic groups in the region.

Is that relevant? I believe that it is. For hundreds, even thousands, of years, my people have been culturally, ethnically, and linguistically distinct from the Persians, Turks, Arabs and others who came into the region. Although our values and needs have been shaped by some of the same factors, I believe that they are not simply the same, and that our identity as a people cannot find its fullest expression in a country that is not our own.

Worse, in those countries where we live, there are consistent attempts to erode the distinctiveness of our ethnicity. I keep returning to the example of Turkey claiming that Kurds did not even exist, but I do so because of its importance. It shows the extent to which people will go in the name of national unity, and the dangers to our culture that exist in the world. We saw in previous chapters the propaganda attempts from Saddam's regime, which tried to redefine what it meant to be Kurdish, and the after effects of the Anfal, which have had dramatic cultural effects on my people, principally by making them far more urbanised.

As has been said again and again by a number of writers, the Kurds remain the largest ethnic group without their own country. I established in chapter one that there are more of my people in the world than in many mid-sized countries, and enough in Iraq to make for a more than valid political unit. Yet this argument seems to be one that is ignored every time my people try to raise it.

Why? Perhaps people are uncomfortable with the idea of countries based on ethnic groups, because that is the language that Nazi Germany used as an initial justification for expansion, citing the idea of bringing in 'Germans' when annexing surrounding territory. Perhaps they feel that in a supposedly multi-cultural world, we should not care about the incompatibilities of ethnic groups within a country, that everybody concerned should try harder to get along, and that ethnicity is not an adequate basis for a state.

If either of these things are what people feel, perhaps they should think again. My people are looking for a country, certainly, but they are not planning on annexing large portions of Kurdistan's neighbours, or even on taking lands 'belonging' to someone else. Kurdistan already exists with well-defined borders. We are simply asking that it have the autonomy of any other sovereign state.

As for any suggestion that ethnicity is not a sufficient basis for a nation, consider the construction of the majority of nations. Generally, they have either been formed through outside conquest, or they have come together from piecemeal elements through a sense of shared identity. When recent Western European nations such as Italy and Germany were forming in the late nineteenth century, forming a national identity was one of the biggest challenges those interested in building them faced.

Or take the creation of several more recent countries, from the Balkan states to several of those in modern Africa or the former Soviet Union. Again and again, there has been a splintering of states where power was used to hold together disparate ethnic groups with no collective sense of identity. Generally, the outcomes for the new countries have been good ones so long as the original country has not attempted to hold onto it with violence.

It is in those situations, as we saw in Serbia in our chapter on genocide, that some of the worst atrocities of recent times have occurred. Looked at like that, I would argue that not only is a sufficiently large and distinct ethnic group sometimes an adequate basis for a separate state, but that in certain situations, it is the only way to avoid violence in the long term.

So, in favour of an independent Kurdistan, we have the desires of my people, the weight of history, and the fact of their separate ethnical and cultural identity from the largely Arab population of the south. To those reasons, I would like to add the sheer unsustainability of my people's current position within Iraq, the capacity of Kurdistan to function as a country, the contribution the act would make to the stability of the region and the effects of the programme of genocide.

Let us be clear: the current position is not one that can continue as it is. Currently, my people do have representation in the Iraqi parliament, but it is not sufficient to allow them to stop laws which seem to be explicit attacks on Kurdistan, such as the insistence on equal representation for each ethnic group in Kirkuk despite a Kurdish majority population there or the loss of large tracts of disputed farmland.[21]

There are, moreover, numerous continuing disputes between the Kurdish Regional Government and Bagdad, many of which appear to be insoluble while Kurdistan remains a part of Iraq. There is the question of what percentage of the budget Kurdistan should receive, and in particular what percentage of revenue from oil and gas. There are issues over territory falling within Kurdistan, and the respective roles of the KRG and Bagdad in defence and other matters.

Essentially, it seems like Bagdad wants to treat Kurdistan as simply one more area of Iraq, to be treated the same as all the others. The problem

---

21   http://www.rudaw.net/english/kurds/5093.html

with that comes when it starts to make decisions in the interests of the Arab majority of Iraq as a whole; a majority that simply does not apply within Kurdistan. The Bagdad government is government by the Arab majority, for the Arab majority. By being ethnically separate, but not a separate country, my people end up ignored and marginalised by the Bagdad government, having decisions dictated to us that are simply not in our interests.

The current arrangement of a semi-autonomous government does something to address that, allowing my people a say over local matters, but ultimately it does not go far enough, because there is no sense of permanence to it. For as long as Kurdistan stays a part of Iraq, there will be an element of pressure from non-Kurdish factions in Bagdad who see the regional government as an anomaly to be pushed aside in the interests of extending the central government's authority. Without full independence, we are like a climber who has climbed a long way, but who has not yet found a ledge to rest on. The moment we stop struggling upwards, we fall.

Yet it is such a small step to independence. As I have discussed elsewhere in this book, Kurdistan is currently a country in all but name. It has its own parliament and its own budget. It has its own sources of income, a sustainable economy, and a rate of growth both economically and in terms of infrastructure that has outstripped Iraq for years. It certainly has the economic capacity to survive as a separate country.

Culturally, it is an even smaller step. Kurdistan has a sense of itself as a separate place, and has had for decades; even before the establishment of the regional government. It has its own broadcasting and educational facilities, its own language... stepping over from Kurdistan to the south of Iraq is already like visiting a foreign country in every meaningful respect, and is certainly no less of a difference than visiting Iran, for example.

Even in terms of international relations, Kurdistan is thriving as much as any country its size. With its own ambassadors, it is able to talk to the world's governments and seek support, as well as offering a great deal to the world. The absence of an official status as a country hampers it somewhat in terms of what it is currently able to achieve, however, because it must currently consider its relations with Bagdad with every interaction. This is not just Kurdistan playing at being a country, either. The USA has received Massoud Barzani, while the UK has a parliamentary committee dedicated to monitoring relations with Kurdistan. When it forgets enough to allow itself, the rest of the world treats Kurdistan as a country too.

Yet how much more could it do with UN recognition? Currently, while it can engage in bilateral relations with countries and make agreements, Kurdistan does not get a seat at the table when it comes to Middle East relations. For anything involving multiple countries, Kurdistan continues to be seen as just a part of Iraq, making it impossible to get Kurdistan's views across in the forums that matter. Worse, without the status that independence would give to it, Kurdistan is not in a position to talk seriously with surrounding countries such as Turkey or Syria. That leaves its relations with those countries in a complex, nebulous and frequently hostile state, rather than in one that is more equal and settled.

Because the recognition of an independent Kurdistan *would* contribute to the stability of the region in the longer term. Yes, there would be initial questions over the exact extent of Kurdistan's borders and which resources fall under its control. There would be arguments over whether Kirkuk should go with the independent country or stay with Iraq. Yet the point is that those arguments are *already* happening. Kurdistan and Bagdad continue to contest these issues, and one of the major arguments involved seems to be about how much Bagdad, as Iraq's central government, should have control over. There is a divide between the power that comes with the technologically advanced military of Kurdistan and the notional authority of Bagdad, and the lack of certainty is damaging for the whole region.

If Kurdistan were independent, those issues would have to be settled between the two countries, but they might finally be settled on a more equal and reasonable basis. More than that, they would be far more permanently settled as an agreement between two countries than as an arrangement between a specific central government and what it sees as one of its regions. Several of the key issues between the two, such as over Kurdish representation, would cease to be issues at all.

I suspect that the region around Kurdistan would become more stable too. Firstly, Kurdistan's relations with a number of surrounding countries would be placed on a more formal footing than the current one where they refuse to acknowledge its existence. That would help to stabilise several borders, as well as make international relations involving the region somewhat less complex, because there wouldn't be the difficulty of trying to talk to Kurdistan unofficially while conducting official relations with Bagdad.

There is also the issue of Kurdish separatist groups in countries such as Syria and Turkey. I know that these countries must be worried that if Kurdistan becomes an independent nation, their populations of Kurds will immediately secede, taking large portions of their border territories with them. Obviously, I am in no position to make promises about the future, but it seems to me that the existence of an independent Kurdistan also has the potential to work the other way.

What do Kurdish separatists in other countries want? They want a separate Kurdish homeland where they will not be persecuted by governments that will never care about them. If such a place already exists in the form of a genuinely independent Kurdistan, will those groups truly want to continue their fight elsewhere? Some might, but it seems likely that many will take the opportunity presented by the new nation. At the very least, an independent Kurdistan will provide nations that are currently engaged in complex and often hostile relations with my people with a real point of contact and negotiation.

So Kurdistan could be an effective independent nation, and I believe that its independence would do a lot to simplify both the domestic and international relations of the region around it. All of these elements are good reasons why Kurdistan should be independent.

They are, however, secondary to the most important factor, which is the genocide that I have spent most of this book exploring.

What happens in the aftermath of genocides? We explored several earlier, and the answer varies. With the genocide in Rwanda, the Tutsi government displayed remarkable forbearance when it came to the Hutu perpetrators of that genocide, offering an amnesty to those return- ing after fleeing the country. That government felt that holding Rwanda together was more important than pursuing revenge, and it must have been a difficult decision to take.

I have used the example of Rwanda first here because it is so unusual. It is a situation that is not replicated in other genocides, and which stems from an unusual set of circumstances, most notably the power reversal that saw a Tutsi government so soon after their persecu- tion. In other situations, things have been far less simple, and the aftermath of genocide has often led to the rearrangement of the interna- tional map. With the Jewish Holocaust, for example, its aftermath saw the creation of Israel. The genocides in the Balkans happened in the context of an existing break-up of the former Yugoslavia, but they helped to deepen the divides involved and bring about a more rapid transition to separate states. South Sudan owes its existence entirely to the danger of genocide, created as a way of protecting its population from the Sudanese government.

Actually, the idea of protecting a people is the key to understanding each of these responses. The creation of new states came out of the need for particular ethnic groups to have enough control over their own lives to keep themselves safe. They needed to determine their own lives, and frequently also to physically separate themselves from the people who had tried to destroy them. Even in Rwanda, that principle of protection applies. The government of Rwanda was able to pursue a policy of reconciliation because it *was* the government. The Tutsi people were in a position of sufficient power to protect themselves from future attacks.

We have seen in this book that the genocide of the mid-1980s connects in to wider issues in Iraq. It connects to lingering tensions between the country's Arab rulers and my people. It connects to a country historically run by Arab rulers for an Arab majority, with my people marginalised and repressed when they sought freedom. It connects in to tactics of repression used by a succession of Arab rulers against my people, even if Saddam Hussein's regime took it far further.

How do my people feel safe after that? After that, how are we meant to turn around and accept the Arab majority of Iraq as our brothers? There seems to be an expectation among the international community, and certainly from the Bagdad government, that Kurdistan should put everything that has happened to one side and do just that. How? I accept that not every Arab wishes to kill me and my people, but please understand that as I grew up, the only Arabs I saw were the soldiers and guards who had come to kill or abuse my people. The same is true for far too many Kurds.

In that situation, how are things meant to return to normal? How are Arabs and Kurds meant to be one country, when there is always that suspicion over whether it will happen again? Whether there will be more village clearances, more deaths and more camps? The men who ordered those things are dead now, but the attitudes that brought them into being are still alive and well. For far too many Arabs, even ones in positions of authority, my people remain a problem to be solved. If Kurdistan's armed forces were not there, can we really say that they would not seek to 'solve' that problem through violence?

I know that this is not what the international community wants to hear. The United States and others want a unified Iraq; one that works without further tensions. They want us, I think, to pretend that everything is fine. I can pretend. I can pretend that the Arab government in Bagdad cares about my people. I can pretend that many of the inhabitants of Iraq wouldn't be happier if my people didn't exist. I can pretend, but the doubts about the safety of my people will not go away just because I pretend. It won't solve the deep divisions between the Kurds and the Arabs. It won't solve any of the lingering issues between Iraq's central government and my people. Issues that have the potential to erupt into violence if they are not dealt with.

I'm sure there are those who will say that nationhood would not solve those problems either, yet the example set by other genocides suggests that it can help. In the years following the Balkan conflicts and their genocides, for example, the countries that formed from the ruins of Yugoslavia were initially hostile to one another. Slowly though, their relations have improved. Why? Because they had the space they needed to feel safe and to grow. The same could be true for Kurdistan. It *should* be true for Kurdistan.

The case for an independent Kurdistan is compelling. As for the case against, I have already addressed many of the key issues, but essentially now, they come down to the need of the Bagdad government to maintain what it sees as its territory, and the desire of the international community to push its plan for the growth and stability of Iraq.

Hopefully by now, I have shown that independence for Kurdistan would actually be a beneficial step for that second goal, as well as for the whole region. As for the notion of Iraq retaining its territory, has Kurdistan ever really been under its control? It certainly isn't now, and hasn't been since 1991. So what is Iraq really losing? The answer to that is the same as it always seems to have been around Kurdistan: the oil and resources in the region, yet really, does the Bagdad government have a realistic prospect of recovering them? And are they really more important than the well-being of an entire people?

The answer must surely be no. Kurdistan is more important than that. It is the homeland of my people, and the one place that they can feel genuinely safe after decades of repression. It is also an idea; a chance for the future. As a region, it has already done so much to heal the wounds of the past, but as a country, I think it could go so much further. I believe that it has the potential to make an important contribution to the world, and that all my people have a duty to ensure that it does so.

I believe that the case for an independent Kurdistan has grown to the point where it is impossible to ignore. It is something my people want, something that would be good for the region, and something that Kurdistan is ready for. I look forward to the day when the rest of the world agrees with me. On that day, I will be able to look around the region that has been my home and finally call it what it really is.

My country.

Glossary

Abu Graib- A prison in the south of Iraq, used by the regime to imprison many Kurds and political opponents. Later taken over by Coalition military forces.

Algiers Accords- The 1975 agreement between Iraq and Iran promising the cessation of hostilities, and particularly the use of peshmerga fighters. The agreement cleared the way for many of the attacks on the Kurds in the late 1970s.

Ali Hassan Al-Majid- (1941-2010) A cousin of Saddam Hussein also known as "Chemical Ali" for his part in the attack on Halabja and the use of chemical weapons elsewhere. He was the regime's commander for Kurdistan during the Anfal, and helped to plan its atrocities.

Anfal- Or the "spoils of war". The 1987-8 campaign by the Iraqi military aimed at the extermination of the Kurds in numerous, mostly rural, areas of Kurdistan. It featured the extensive use of chemical weapons, notably at Halabja, but also the systematic destruction of villages and the imprisonment or murder of all Kurds found.

Arabization- The policy of introducing Arabs and Arab culture to Kurdistan to strengthen the Bagdad regime's control over the region. It included Arabic teaching in schools, the giving of land to Arabs who were persuaded to resettle, and an emphasis on Arabic culture as the default throughout Iraq.

Ba'ath- The ruling party of Iraq from 1968-2003, and currently the ruling party in Syria. Socialist and Pan Arabic in its doctrines. Officially headed by Saddam Hussein in Iraq from 1979, although he had de-facto control from 1976.

Baherka Camp- One of the camps around Erbil used to contain captured Barzani. The camp in which I spent the majority of my childhood.

Barzani- The tribe within the Kurds to which I belong, and which has traditionally been strongly in favour Kurdish autonomy. Barzani men and boys were targeted in the 1983 mass murders, while Barzani leaders such as General Mullah Mustafa Barzani have been key figures in the resistance to rule from Bagdad. Traditionally, Barzani men are identifiable by red and white scarves, worn in pairs by Barzani family members.

Massoud Barzani- General Mullah Mustafa Barzani's son, responsible for maintaining a government in exile during much of the persecution of my people and for leading the defence of the freed Kurds in the 1990s.

The president of the Kurdistan Regional

Government at the time of writing.

General Mullah Mustafa Barzani- Arguably the most important figure in the struggle for Kurdish independence and highly revered by my people. He led numerous revolts against outside rule, including those of 1945, 1963-6 and 1968. He was involved in the establishment of the Republic of Mahabad in 1945-6, and spent time exiled in the Soviet Union after that country withdrew its support a year later. The peace accords of 1971 that he helped to negotiate ultimately failed, but the principles of separate governance for the region that they contained helped to pave the way for the current region of Kurdistan.

Dohuk- One of Kurdistan's main cities, in the North-West of the region, and capital of an administrative area centred on the city. Also spelled Duhok. Its university, originally opened by volunteers using former regime facilities, is often seen as symbolic of the spirit of rebuilding in Kurdistan.

Erbil- Sometimes known as Arbil or Hawler (in reference to the city's ancient name), this city stands roughly in the centre of Kurdistan and is home to the KRG as well as being at the heart of its own administrative unit. One of the largest cities in Kurdistan, it is also home to Erbil International Airport, Kurdistan's first international airport and one of many key infrastructure projects undertaken in the region.

Germian Plain- An area South East of Kirkuk. The principal target of the third phase of the Anfal.

Halabja- A city close to the Iran-Iraq border. Targeted by the regime with chemical weapons on the 16th March 1988 as part of the Anfal. One of the only attacks on a city during this campaign, with around 3,000-5,000 civilian deaths.

Harir Camp- One of the camps established for the containment of the Kurds, and specifically the Barzani, around Erbil in the late 1970s.

Saddam Hussein- (1937-2006) Former dictator of Iraq. Had de-facto control of the country from 1976, and official control from 1979. The driving force behind the genocide of the Kurds. Despite that, his execution was for a number of earlier murders, and he never faced trial for genocide.

Iraqi Kurdistan- Northern, largely autonomous region of Iraq, taking in cities including Erbil, Sulaymaniyah, Dohuk and Kirkuk. With an independent government, its own flag, anthem and ambassadors, it is a country in all but name. Not to be confused with the wider area of Kurdistan, spread across several countries, where the population is predominantly Kurdish but divided by national borders.

Jash- A slang term referring to those Kurds

who served in the Iraqi army.

Kirkuk- A city in the south of Kurdistan, noted for its oil reserves. Those reserves have made it the object of numerous disputes, and the target for extensive policies of Arabization.

KRG- The Kurdistan Regional Government. The democratically elected government of the region, currently based in Erbil.

Mahabad Republic- The short lived Kurdish homeland created in 1941 Northern Iran, under Qazi Muhammed. It failed in 1946 when the Soviet Union withdrew military support, leaving it open to attack from those who did not wish it to exist. Many of those involved in the republic were subsequently executed, but General Mullah Mustafa Barzani and three hundred followers were able to escape to the Soviet Union.

OPEC- Organisation of Petroleum Exporting Countries. A trans-national organisation composed of those countries engaged in the export of oil. Since Iran and Iraq are both members, several important negotiations have taken place during OPEC summits.

Peshmerga- Kurdish freedom fighters/irregular soldiers, often forced to use guerrilla tactics due to the heavier weaponry, artillery and air superiority of the regime's forces. They were key in helping Kurdistan break free of Saddam's control.

PDK- The Kurdistan Democracy Party. Kurdistan's main political party during the period covered by this book, founded by General Mullah Mustafa Barzani. His son, Massoud Barzani, is the party's current leader, as well as the president of the Kurdistan Regional Government.

PUK- The Patriotic Union Kurdistan. Another of Kurdistan's major political parties.

Qara Dagh- An area of Kurdistan. The subject of the earliest phase of the Anfal.

Qush Tappa Camp- One of the camps around Erbil created to contain the Barzani in the late 1970s.

Seberan Camp- A camp in which my family was initially imprisoned before being moved on to the Baherka camp. One of the camps used to contain the Barzani from the late 1970s, it seems to have initially served as a temporary facility, before the subsequent division of the Barzani between other camps.

Sherwan- The village in which I was born. Destroyed in the 1978 village clearances that were a precursor to the later genocides.

Sulaymaniyah- One of Kurdistan's main cities, in the East of the region. Controls the administrative district of the same name, and has more than 1.5 million inhabitants. It is often seen as one of the most important cultural centres in Kurdistan.

As with the region's other major cities, it has undergone extensive rebuilding in recent years.

Treaty of Lausanne- A treaty signed in Switzerland in 1923. It effectively overturned the promises of the Treaty of Sevres, creating modern Iraq and failing to provide land for an independent Kurdish state.

Treaty of Sevres- A treaty of 1920, between the Ottoman Empire and the Allies of World War One. Its terms included provisions for the later creation of a Kurdish homeland, but those were never put into practice.

Yezidism- A religion rarely found outside Kurdistan, related to Kurdistan's pre-Muslim beliefs.

Further Reading

Arburish, Said K, *Saddam Hussein: The Politics of Revenge* (Bloomsbury, New York, 2000)

Bengio, Ofra, "The Iraqi Kurds: The Struggle for Autonomy in the Shadow of the Iran-Iraqi Conflict" *Immigrants and Minorities,* vol. 9, no. 3 (November 1990) pp249-68

Bird, Christiane, *A Thousand Sighs, A Thousand Revolts* (Random House, New York, 2005)

Bullock, John and Harvey Morris, *No Friends But the Mountains: The Tragic History of the Kurds,* (Oxford University Press, 1992)

Bruinessen, Martin van, *Kurdish Ethno-Nationalism Versus Nation-Building States* (Isis Press, Istanbul, 2000)

Chaliand, Gerard (ed), *A People Without a Country: The Kurds and Kurdistan,* (Olive Branch Press, New York, 1993)

Charney, Israel W. (ed) *Genocide: A Critical Bibliographical Review,* (Mansell, London, 1988)

Cockburn, Andrew and Patrick Cockburn, *Out of the Ashes: The Resurrection of Saddam Hussein,* (HarperCollins, New York, 1999)

Dodge, Toby, *Inventing Iraq: The Failure of Nation Building and a History Denied,* (Columbia Press, New York, 2003)

Fromkin, David, *A Peace to End All Peace: The Fall of the Ottoman Empire and the Creation of the Modern Middle East*, (Henry Holt and Co, New York, 1989)

Gutman, Roy and David Rieff (eds), *Crimes of War: What the Public Should Know* (Norton, New York, 1999)

Hiltermann, Joost R, *A Poisonous Affair*, (Cambridge University Press, 2007)

Hiltermann, Joost R, "Kirkuk and the Kurds: A Difficult Choice Ahead", (International Crisis Group, 2007)

Hiltermann, Joost R, "Of Blood, Oil and Kurdistan" (International Crisis Group, 2011)

Human Rights Watch, *Genocide in Iraq: The Anfal Campaign Against the Kurds*, (Human Rights Watch, New York, 1993, 2006)

Human Rights Watch, *Syria: The Silenced Kurds*, (Human Rights Watch, New York, 1996)

Kreyenbroek, Philip G, and Stefan Sperl, (eds), *The Kurds: A Contemporary Overview*, (Routledge, London, 1992)

Laizer, Sheri, *Martyrs, Traitors and Patriots: Kurdistan After the Gulf War* (Zed Books, New Jersey, 1996) Lawrence, Quil, *Invisible Nation*, (Walker and Company, New York, 2008)

Lennox, Gina (ed), *Snow and Honey: Voices from Kurdistan* (Halstead Press, New South Wales, 2001)

Makiya, Kanan, *The Republic of Fear: The Politics of Modern Iraq* (University of California Press, 1998)

McDowall, David, *The Kurds: A Nation Denied* (Minority Rights Publications, London, 1992)

Meiselas, Susan, *Kurdistan: In the Shadow of History*, (Random House, New York, 1997)

Middle East Watch, *Human Rights in Iraq*, (Yale University Press, 1990)

Miller, Judith, "Iraq Accused: A Case of Genocide" *New York Times Magazine* (3rd of January 1993) pp12-17, 28, 31-36

Winds of Death: Iraq's Use of Poison Gas against its Kurdish Population, (Physicians for Human Rights, 1989)

Power, Samantha, *A Problem From Hell: America and the Age of Genocide* (Basic Books, New York, 2002)

Randal, Jonathan C, *After Such Knowledge, What Forgiveness: My Encounters with Kurdistan,* (Farrar, Straus and Giroux, New York, 1997)

Schuurman, Susan J, *An Inconvenient Atrocity*, (University of New Mexico, 2007)

Talabany, Nouri, *Arabization of the Kirkuk Region,* (Khak Press, London, 1999)

About the author

Davan is a political activist and supporter of the PDK (Partîya Demokrata Kurdistan – Kurdistan Democratic Party). Born on the 1st July, 1974 in a small Village called Sherwan in the Barzan region of Iraqi Kurdistan, he was resettled from his home by Saddam Hussein's regime in the 1980s. There he witnessed the atrocities inflicted upon his people first-hand. Forced to leave his homeland in 1993 like many of his countrymen he started a new life in the UK. He continued his fight against Saddam by raising awareness for his people and their plight. This book is an insight into the oppression suffered, the struggle endured and an optimistic feeling for the future of modern Kurdistan.

Picture Section

The modern city of Erbil at night

Typical Kurdish tea shop 1973

Baherka camp where I lived
from 1978 to 1993

President Barzani addresses the crowd at
the Erbil Citadel in commemoration of the
20th anniversary of their liberation from
Saddam's dictatorial rule

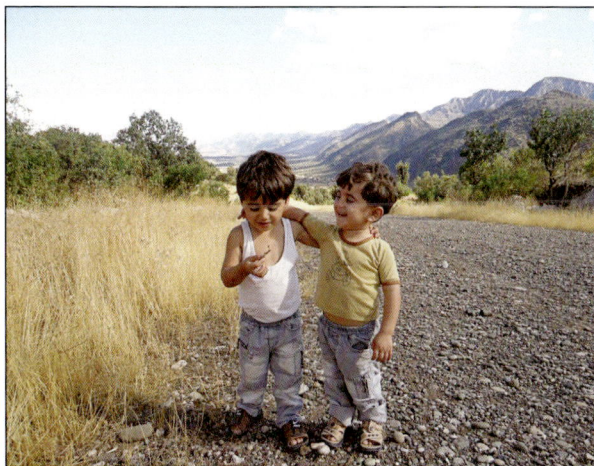

Two local boys in the Barzan region

Kurdish boy in Peshmerga uniform

City of Sulaimaniya

Halabja memorial, in commemoration of the gas attacks by Saddam Hussain's army, on March 16, 1988, killing about 5,000 of its citizens, and injuring nearly 20,000

Halabja Cemetery

General Mullah Mustafa Barzani, Northern Iraq,
Spring 1965 (remastered)

General Mullah Mustafa Barzani